EMIRATI
COOKBOOK

Traditional Recipes from UAE

LIAM LUXE

.

CONTENTS

INTRODUCTION

Emirati means it's from the United Arab Emirates, a cool place with lots of great flavors.

Inside this book, you'll find authentic Emirati recipes, making delicious dishes that mix flavors from different places. There are tasty things with spices, yummy meats, fragrant rice, and sweet desserts – everything that makes Emirati food special.

You can use this cookbook for different adventures in your kitchen. Whether you want to make something special for family time or impress your friends with unique dishes, these recipes have got you covered.

People in the Emirates have been making these dishes for a long, long time. The recipes are like secrets passed down from grandparents to parents and now to you. It's like a yummy time machine!

While these recipes are a guide, feel free to add your own touch. Cooking is like painting – you can make it your own masterpiece. Happy cooking!

APPETIZERS AND SNACKS

AL HAREES SAMOSAS

Servings: 12 samosas
Time: 1.5 hours

Ingredients:

- 1 cup cooked Al Harees (leftover or freshly made)
- 2 cups finely chopped cooked chicken
- 1 cup finely chopped onions
- 1 teaspoon ground cumin
- 1 teaspoon ground coriander
- Salt to taste
- 2 tablespoons chopped fresh cilantro
- 12 samosa wrappers (store-bought or homemade)

Instructions:

1. In a bowl, mix Al Harees, cooked chicken, onions, cumin, coriander, salt, and cilantro.
2. Take a samosa wrapper and fold it into a cone shape, sealing the edge with water.
3. Fill the cone with the Al Harees and chicken mixture, sealing the open edge with water.
4. Repeat for all samosas.
5. Heat oil in a pan over medium heat.
6. Fry samosas until golden brown and crispy.
7. Drain excess oil on paper towels.
8. Serve hot with your favorite chutney or dipping sauce.

FALAFEL WITH TAHINI SAUCE

Servings: 20 falafel
Time: 1.5 hours

Ingredients:

- 2 cups dried chickpeas, soaked overnight
- 1 small onion, roughly chopped
- 3 cloves garlic
- 1 cup fresh parsley, chopped
- 1 teaspoon ground cumin
- 1 teaspoon ground coriander
- 1 teaspoon baking powder
- Salt to taste
- 4 tablespoons all-purpose flour
- Oil for frying

Tahini Sauce:

- 1/2 cup tahini
- 1/4 cup water
- 2 tablespoons lemon juice
- 1 clove garlic, minced
- Salt to taste

Instructions:

1. Rinse soaked chickpeas and place them in a food processor.
2. Add onion, garlic, parsley, cumin, coriander, baking powder, salt, and flour. Blend until a coarse mixture forms.
3. Shape the mixture into small balls or patties.
4. Heat oil in a pan over medium heat.
5. Fry falafel until golden brown and crispy.
6. For tahini sauce, mix tahini, water, lemon juice, minced garlic, and salt in a bowl.
7. Serve falafel hot with tahini sauce for dipping.

STUFFED GRAPE LEAVES (WARAK ENAB)

Servings: 30 stuffed grape leaves
Time: 1.5 hours

Ingredients:

- 1 cup grape leaves, preserved in brine
- 1 cup short-grain rice, rinsed
- 1/2 cup minced onions
- 1/4 cup pine nuts
- 1/4 cup chopped fresh dill
- 1/4 cup chopped fresh mint

- 1/4 cup lemon juice
- 2 tablespoons olive oil
- Salt and pepper to taste
- Water for boiling

Instructions:

1. Boil grape leaves for 2 minutes to soften. Drain and set aside.
2. In a bowl, mix rice, minced onions, pine nuts, dill, mint, lemon juice, olive oil, salt, and pepper.
3. Place a grape leaf flat on a surface, shiny side down.
4. Spoon a small amount of the rice mixture onto the center of the leaf.
5. Fold the sides of the leaf over the filling, then roll it up tightly.
6. Repeat for all grape leaves.
7. Arrange stuffed grape leaves in a pot, seam side down.
8. Pour enough water to cover the grape leaves.
9. Place a heavy plate on top to keep them from unraveling.
10. Simmer over low heat for 45 minutes to 1 hour.
11. Allow to cool before serving.

CHEESE FATAYER

Servings: 12 fatayers
Time: 1.5 hours

Dough:

- 2 cups all-purpose flour
- 1 tablespoon yeast
- 1 tablespoon sugar

- 1/2 cup warm water
- 1/4 cup olive oil
- 1/2 teaspoon salt

Cheese Filling:

- 1 cup feta cheese, crumbled
- 1 cup ricotta cheese
- 1/4 cup chopped fresh parsley
- 1/4 teaspoon black pepper

Instructions:

1. In a bowl, dissolve yeast and sugar in warm water. Let it sit until frothy.
2. In a large bowl, mix flour and salt. Add the yeast mixture and olive oil.
3. Knead the dough until smooth. Cover and let it rise for 1 hour.
4. Preheat the oven to 375°F (190°C).
5. In a separate bowl, combine feta cheese, ricotta cheese, parsley, and black pepper for the filling.
6. Divide the dough into 12 portions.
7. Roll each portion into a small circle.
8. Place a spoonful of the cheese mixture in the center of each circle.
9. Fold the edges of the dough over the filling, forming a triangle.
10. Pinch the edges to seal the fatayer.
11. Place the fatayers on a baking sheet.
12. Bake for 15-20 minutes or until golden brown.
13. Allow to cool slightly before serving.

KEBBEH NAYEH (RAW MEAT KEBBEH)

Servings: 4 servings
Time: 30 minutes

Ingredients:

- 1 pound lean ground beef or lamb
- 1 cup fine bulgur, soaked in water
- 1 small onion, finely chopped
- 1/4 cup fresh mint, finely chopped
- 1/4 cup fresh parsley, finely chopped
- 1/4 teaspoon ground cinnamon
- Salt to taste
- Olive oil for drizzling
- Ice cubes for serving

Instructions:

1. Drain the soaked bulgur and squeeze out excess water.
2. In a bowl, mix ground meat, bulgur, chopped onion, mint, parsley, cinnamon, and salt.
3. Blend the mixture thoroughly until it becomes a smooth paste.
4. Spread the meat mixture on a serving plate, creating an even surface.
5. Using the back of a spoon, create decorative patterns on the surface.
6. Drizzle olive oil over the top.
7. Serve immediately, accompanied by ice cubes to keep it cool.

SPINACH AND CHEESE SAMBOUSEK

Servings: 20 sambousek
Time: 1 hour

Dough:

- 2 cups all-purpose flour
- 1/2 cup unsalted butter, melted
- 1/2 cup plain yogurt
- 1/2 teaspoon baking powder
- 1/4 teaspoon salt

Filling:

- 2 cups fresh spinach, chopped
- 1 cup feta cheese, crumbled
- 1/2 cup mozzarella cheese, shredded
- 1 small onion, finely chopped
- 1 teaspoon olive oil
- Salt and pepper to taste

Instructions:

1. Preheat the oven to 375°F (190°C).
2. In a large bowl, combine flour, melted butter, yogurt, baking powder, and salt. Knead until a soft dough forms.
3. In a pan, sauté chopped spinach and onion in olive oil until wilted. Allow to cool.
4. Mix feta cheese, mozzarella cheese, sautéed spinach, and onions. Season with salt and pepper.
5. Roll out portions of the dough into small circles.
6. Place a spoonful of the spinach and cheese mixture in the center of each circle.
7. Fold the dough over the filling, forming a semi-circle, and press the edges to seal.

8. Place the sambousek on a baking sheet.
9. Bake for 15-20 minutes or until golden brown.
10. Allow to cool slightly before serving.

CHICKEN SHAWARMA ROLLS

Servings: 4 rolls
Time: 1 hour

Marinade:

- 1 pound boneless, skinless chicken thighs
- 3 cloves garlic, minced
- 1 teaspoon ground cumin
- 1 teaspoon ground coriander
- 1 teaspoon smoked paprika
- 1 teaspoon ground turmeric
- 1 teaspoon ground cinnamon
- Salt and black pepper to taste
- 2 tablespoons plain yogurt
- 2 tablespoons olive oil
- Juice of 1 lemon

Tahini Sauce:

- 1/2 cup tahini
- 2 tablespoons lemon juice
- 1 clove garlic, minced
- Salt to taste
- Water (as needed for thinning)

Assembly:

- 4 large flatbreads or tortillas
- Sliced tomatoes
- Sliced cucumbers
- Chopped lettuce
- Pickles (optional)

Instructions:

1. In a bowl, mix all the marinade ingredients.
2. Slice chicken thighs into thin strips and coat them in the marinade. Let it marinate for at least 30 minutes.
3. Cook the marinated chicken in a skillet over medium-high heat until fully cooked.
4. In a separate bowl, whisk together tahini, lemon juice, minced garlic, and salt. Add water as needed to achieve a drizzling consistency.
5. Warm the flatbreads or tortillas.
6. Assemble the rolls by placing a generous portion of cooked chicken in the center of each bread.
7. Top with sliced tomatoes, cucumbers, lettuce, and pickles if desired.
8. Drizzle tahini sauce over the filling.
9. Roll the bread tightly around the filling, forming a shawarma roll.

MUHAMMARA (RED PEPPER AND WALNUT DIP)

Servings: 1.5 cups
Time: 15 minutes

Ingredients:

- 2 large red bell peppers, roasted and peeled
- 1 cup walnuts, toasted
- 2 cloves garlic, minced
- 2 tablespoons olive oil
- 1 tablespoon pomegranate molasses
- 1 teaspoon ground cumin
- 1/2 teaspoon red pepper flakes (adjust to taste)
- Salt to taste

Instructions:

1. Roast red bell peppers until charred, then peel and remove seeds.
2. In a food processor, combine roasted red peppers, toasted walnuts, minced garlic, olive oil, pomegranate molasses, ground cumin, red pepper flakes, and salt.
3. Blend until smooth, scraping down the sides as needed.
4. Taste and adjust the seasoning, adding more salt or red pepper flakes if desired.
5. Transfer the muhammara to a serving bowl.
6. Drizzle with a bit of olive oil and garnish with chopped walnuts or parsley if desired.
7. Serve as a dip with pita bread, crackers, or fresh vegetables.

MOUTABAL (EGGPLANT DIP)

Servings: 1.5 cups
Time: 40 minutes

Ingredients:

- 1 large eggplant

- 2 tablespoons tahini
- 2 cloves garlic, minced
- Juice of 1 lemon
- 2 tablespoons olive oil
- Salt and pepper to taste
- Chopped fresh parsley for garnish

Instructions:

1. Preheat the oven to 400°F (200°C).
2. Prick the eggplant with a fork and place it on a baking sheet.
3. Roast the eggplant in the oven for 30-40 minutes or until the skin is charred and the inside is soft.
4. Allow the eggplant to cool, then peel off the charred skin.
5. In a bowl, mash the eggplant with a fork or blend for a smoother consistency.
6. Add tahini, minced garlic, lemon juice, olive oil, salt, and pepper to the mashed eggplant. Mix well.
7. Adjust seasoning to taste, adding more tahini or lemon juice if desired.
8. Transfer the moutabal to a serving dish, drizzle with olive oil, and garnish with chopped parsley.
9. Serve with pita bread or vegetable sticks for dipping.

LAMB SAMBOUSEK

Servings: 20 sambousek
Time: 1.5 hours

Dough:

- 2 cups all-purpose flour

- 1/2 cup unsalted butter, melted
- 1/2 cup plain yogurt
- 1/2 teaspoon baking powder
- 1/4 teaspoon salt

Lamb Filling:

- 1/2 pound ground lamb
- 1 small onion, finely chopped
- 2 tablespoons pine nuts
- 1 teaspoon ground cinnamon
- 1/2 teaspoon ground allspice
- Salt and pepper to taste

Instructions:

1. Preheat the oven to 375°F (190°C).
2. In a large bowl, combine flour, melted butter, yogurt, baking powder, and salt. Knead until a soft dough forms.
3. In a pan, cook ground lamb over medium heat until browned.
4. Add chopped onion, pine nuts, ground cinnamon, allspice, salt, and pepper to the lamb. Cook until onions are soft.
5. Roll out portions of the dough into small circles.
6. Place a spoonful of the lamb mixture in the center of each circle.
7. Fold the dough over the filling, forming a semi-circle, and press the edges to seal.
8. Place the sambousek on a baking sheet.
9. Bake for 15-20 minutes or until golden brown.
10. Allow to cool slightly before serving.

SOUPS AND SALADS

LENTIL SOUP

Servings: 6 bowls
Time: 45 minutes

Ingredients:

- 1 cup dried brown lentils, rinsed
- 1 large onion, finely chopped
- 2 carrots, diced
- 2 celery stalks, diced
- 3 cloves garlic, minced
- 1 teaspoon ground cumin
- 1 teaspoon ground coriander
- 1/2 teaspoon turmeric
- 6 cups vegetable or chicken broth

- Salt and pepper to taste
- Olive oil for drizzling
- Fresh parsley for garnish

Instructions:

1. In a large pot, sauté chopped onion, carrots, and celery in olive oil until softened.
2. Add minced garlic, ground cumin, ground coriander, and turmeric. Stir for 1-2 minutes until fragrant.
3. Add rinsed lentils and broth to the pot.
4. Bring to a boil, then reduce heat and simmer for 25-30 minutes or until lentils are tender.
5. Use an immersion blender to partially blend the soup for a thicker consistency.
6. Season with salt and pepper to taste.
7. Serve hot, drizzled with olive oil and garnished with fresh parsley.

FATTOUSH SALAD

Servings: 4 bowls
Time: 20 minutes

Ingredients:

- 4 cups mixed salad greens (lettuce, arugula, radicchio)
- 1 cup cherry tomatoes, halved
- 1 cucumber, diced
- 1 bell pepper, diced
- 1/2 red onion, thinly sliced
- 1 cup radishes, thinly sliced
- 1/2 cup fresh mint leaves

- 1/2 cup fresh parsley, chopped
- 1 cup toasted pita bread, broken into bite-sized pieces

Dressing:

- 1/4 cup olive oil
- 2 tablespoons lemon juice
- 1 teaspoon ground sumac
- 1 teaspoon pomegranate molasses
- Salt and pepper to taste

Instructions:

1. In a large bowl, combine mixed salad greens, cherry tomatoes, cucumber, bell pepper, red onion, radishes, mint, parsley, and toasted pita bread.
2. In a small bowl, whisk together olive oil, lemon juice, ground sumac, pomegranate molasses, salt, and pepper to create the dressing.
3. Drizzle the dressing over the salad and toss gently to coat evenly.
4. Allow the salad to sit for a few minutes to let the flavors meld.
5. Serve immediately, ensuring each portion includes a mix of all the colorful ingredients.

FREEKEH SALAD WITH ROASTED VEGETABLES

Servings: 4 bowls
Time: 40 minutes

Ingredients:

- 1 cup freekeh, cooked and cooled
- 2 cups mixed vegetables (zucchini, cherry tomatoes, bell peppers), chopped
- 1 red onion, thinly sliced
- 1 cup chickpeas, cooked (canned or boiled)
- 1/4 cup fresh parsley, chopped
- 2 tablespoons olive oil
- 1 teaspoon ground cumin
- 1 teaspoon ground coriander
- Salt and pepper to taste

Dressing:

- 3 tablespoons olive oil
- 2 tablespoons balsamic vinegar
- 1 tablespoon honey
- 1 teaspoon Dijon mustard
- Salt and pepper to taste

Instructions:

1. Preheat the oven to 400°F (200°C).
2. In a baking dish, toss the mixed vegetables with olive oil, ground cumin, ground coriander, salt, and pepper.
3. Roast the vegetables in the oven for 20-25 minutes or until they are golden and slightly charred.
4. In a large bowl, combine cooked freekeh, roasted vegetables, red onion, chickpeas, and fresh parsley.
5. In a small bowl, whisk together olive oil, balsamic vinegar, honey, Dijon mustard, salt, and pepper to create the dressing.
6. Drizzle the dressing over the salad and toss gently to combine.

7. Allow the flavors to mingle for a few minutes before serving.

AL MARQOQ (OKRA SOUP)

Servings: 4 bowls
Time: 45 minutes

Ingredients:

- 1 pound fresh okra, washed and trimmed
- 1 cup lamb or beef, cubed
- 1 large onion, finely chopped
- 3 tomatoes, diced
- 3 cloves garlic, minced
- 1 teaspoon ground cumin
- 1 teaspoon ground coriander
- 1/2 teaspoon turmeric
- 6 cups chicken or vegetable broth
- Salt and pepper to taste
- 2 tablespoons olive oil
- Lemon wedges for serving

Instructions:

1. Heat olive oil in a pot over medium heat.
2. Sauté chopped onion and minced garlic until softened.
3. Add cubed meat and brown on all sides.
4. Stir in ground cumin, ground coriander, and turmeric until fragrant.
5. Add diced tomatoes and cook until they release their juices.
6. Pour in chicken or vegetable broth and bring to a boil.

7. Add fresh okra to the pot and simmer until the okra is tender, about 20-25 minutes.
8. Season the soup with salt and pepper to taste.
9. Serve hot with lemon wedges on the side.

TABBOULEH

Servings: 4 bowls
Time: 30 minutes

Ingredients:

- 1 cup finely chopped fresh parsley
- 1/2 cup bulgur, soaked in hot water and drained
- 1/2 cup cherry tomatoes, finely chopped
- 1/4 cup fresh mint leaves, finely chopped
- 1/2 cup cucumber, finely diced
- 1/4 cup red onion, finely chopped
- Juice of 2 lemons
- 3 tablespoons olive oil
- Salt and pepper to taste

Instructions:

1. In a large bowl, combine finely chopped parsley, soaked bulgur, cherry tomatoes, fresh mint, diced cucumber, and chopped red onion.
2. In a small bowl, whisk together lemon juice, olive oil, salt, and pepper to create the dressing.
3. Pour the dressing over the tabbouleh mixture and toss gently to combine.
4. Allow the flavors to meld for at least 15 minutes before serving.

5. Taste and adjust the seasoning if needed.

HARIRA (LENTIL AND CHICKPEA SOUP)

Servings: 6 bowls
Time: 1 hour

Ingredients:

- 1 cup dried red lentils, rinsed
- 1 cup cooked chickpeas (canned or boiled)
- 1 large onion, finely chopped
- 2 carrots, diced
- 2 celery stalks, diced
- 3 cloves garlic, minced
- 1 teaspoon ground cumin
- 1 teaspoon ground coriander
- 1/2 teaspoon ground cinnamon
- 1/2 teaspoon ground turmeric
- 1/4 teaspoon cayenne pepper (optional)
- 1 can (14 oz) diced tomatoes
- 6 cups vegetable or chicken broth
- 1/4 cup fresh cilantro, chopped
- 1/4 cup fresh parsley, chopped
- Juice of 1 lemon
- Salt and pepper to taste
- Olive oil for drizzling

Instructions:

1. In a large pot, sauté chopped onion, carrots, and celery in olive oil until softened.

2. Add minced garlic, ground cumin, ground coriander, ground cinnamon, ground turmeric, and cayenne pepper (if using). Stir for 1-2 minutes until fragrant.
3. Add rinsed lentils, cooked chickpeas, diced tomatoes, and broth to the pot.
4. Bring to a boil, then reduce heat and simmer for 30-40 minutes or until lentils are tender.
5. Stir in chopped cilantro, parsley, and lemon juice.
6. Season with salt and pepper to taste.
7. Serve hot, drizzled with olive oil.

CUCUMBER AND MINT YOGURT SALAD

Servings: 4 bowls
Time: 15 minutes

Ingredients:

- 2 cucumbers, thinly sliced
- 1 cup Greek yogurt
- 2 tablespoons fresh mint, finely chopped
- 1 clove garlic, minced
- 1 tablespoon olive oil
- 1 tablespoon lemon juice
- Salt and pepper to taste

Instructions:

1. In a bowl, combine thinly sliced cucumbers and chopped fresh mint.
2. In a separate bowl, whisk together Greek yogurt, minced garlic, olive oil, lemon juice, salt, and pepper.
3. Pour the yogurt mixture over the cucumbers and mint.

4. Toss gently to coat the cucumber slices evenly.
5. Adjust the seasoning to taste.
6. Refrigerate for at least 10 minutes before serving to allow flavors to meld.

BABA GANOUSH SALAD

Servings: 4 bowls
Time: 30 minutes

Ingredients:

- 2 medium-sized eggplants
- 1/4 cup tahini
- 2 cloves garlic, minced
- Juice of 1 lemon
- 2 tablespoons olive oil
- Salt and pepper to taste
- 1/4 cup fresh parsley, chopped
- 1/4 cup cherry tomatoes, halved
- 1/4 cup red bell pepper, finely chopped
- 1/4 cup cucumber, diced
- 1/4 cup red onion, finely sliced
- 1/4 cup Kalamata olives, pitted and sliced (optional)

Instructions:

1. Preheat the oven to 400°F (200°C).
2. Roast the eggplants in the oven until the skin is charred and the flesh is soft, about 25-30 minutes.
3. Allow the eggplants to cool, then peel off the charred skin.

4. Mash the eggplant flesh in a bowl and add tahini, minced garlic, lemon juice, olive oil, salt, and pepper. Mix well.
5. In a separate bowl, combine chopped parsley, halved cherry tomatoes, finely chopped red bell pepper, diced cucumber, sliced red onion, and Kalamata olives (if using).
6. Pour the eggplant mixture over the vegetables and toss gently to combine.
7. Adjust the seasoning to taste.
8. Refrigerate for at least 15 minutes to allow the flavors to meld.

CHICKPEA AND SPINACH STEW

Servings: 4 bowls
Time: 40 minutes

Ingredients:

- 1 can (15 oz) chickpeas, drained and rinsed
- 1 onion, finely chopped
- 2 cloves garlic, minced
- 1 teaspoon ground cumin
- 1 teaspoon ground coriander
- 1/2 teaspoon paprika
- 1/4 teaspoon cayenne pepper
- 1 can (14 oz) diced tomatoes
- 4 cups fresh spinach leaves
- 1 cup vegetable broth
- Salt and pepper to taste
- Olive oil for sautéing

Instructions:

1. In a pot, sauté chopped onion and minced garlic in olive oil until softened.
2. Add ground cumin, ground coriander, paprika, and cayenne pepper. Stir for 1-2 minutes until fragrant.
3. Pour in diced tomatoes with their juice and cook for an additional 3-4 minutes.
4. Add chickpeas, fresh spinach, and vegetable broth to the pot. Stir to combine.
5. Bring the stew to a simmer and cook for 20-25 minutes until flavors meld and spinach wilts.
6. Season with salt and pepper to taste.

LAMB AND VEGETABLE SOUP

Servings: 6 bowls
Time: 1.5 hours

Ingredients:

- 1 pound lamb, cubed
- 1 large onion, finely chopped
- 2 carrots, diced
- 2 celery stalks, diced
- 3 cloves garlic, minced
- 2 potatoes, peeled and diced
- 1 cup green beans, chopped
- 1 can (14 oz) diced tomatoes
- 8 cups beef or lamb broth
- 1 teaspoon dried thyme
- 1 teaspoon dried rosemary
- Salt and pepper to taste
- Olive oil for sautéing

Instructions:

1. In a large pot, brown lamb cubes in olive oil over medium-high heat.
2. Add chopped onion, diced carrots, diced celery, and minced garlic. Sauté until vegetables are softened.
3. Stir in diced potatoes, chopped green beans, and diced tomatoes with their juice.
4. Pour in beef or lamb broth and add dried thyme and dried rosemary.
5. Bring the soup to a boil, then reduce heat and simmer for 1 hour or until lamb is tender.
6. Season with salt and pepper to taste.

RICE AND GRAIN DISHES

MACHBOOS (SPICED RICE WITH MEAT)

Servings: 6 servings
Time: 1.5 hours

Ingredients:

- 2 cups basmati rice, soaked and drained
- 1 pound meat (chicken, lamb, or beef), cubed
- 2 large onions, thinly sliced
- 3 tomatoes, chopped
- 1/4 cup vegetable oil
- 2 tablespoons clarified butter (ghee)
- 4 cloves garlic, minced
- 2 teaspoons ground coriander
- 2 teaspoons ground cumin

- 1 teaspoon ground cinnamon
- 1 teaspoon ground cardamom
- 1 teaspoon ground turmeric
- 1 teaspoon ground black lime (loomi) or substitute with lime zest
- 2 bay leaves
- 4 cups chicken or beef broth
- Salt and pepper to taste
- Fresh coriander or parsley for garnish

Instructions:

1. In a large pot, heat vegetable oil and clarified butter over medium heat.
2. Sauté thinly sliced onions until golden brown and crispy. Remove half for garnish.
3. Add minced garlic to the pot and cook until fragrant.
4. Add meat cubes and brown on all sides.
5. Stir in ground coriander, ground cumin, ground cinnamon, ground cardamom, ground turmeric, and ground black lime (loomi).
6. Add chopped tomatoes and cook until they release their juices.
7. Pour in soaked and drained basmati rice, stirring to coat the rice with the spices.
8. Add bay leaves, then pour in chicken or beef broth. Season with salt and pepper to taste.
9. Bring the mixture to a boil, then reduce heat, cover, and simmer for 20-25 minutes or until the rice is cooked and the liquid is absorbed.
10. Allow the Machboos to rest for a few minutes, then fluff the rice with a fork.

11. Serve hot, garnished with the reserved crispy onions and fresh coriander or parsley.

JAREESH

Servings: 4 servings
Time: 1 hour

Ingredients:

- 1 cup jareesh (cracked wheat)
- 1/2 cup lean lamb or chicken, diced
- 1 large onion, finely chopped
- 2 tomatoes, chopped
- 3 cloves garlic, minced
- 2 tablespoons vegetable oil
- 1 teaspoon ground cumin
- 1 teaspoon ground coriander
- 1/2 teaspoon ground cinnamon
- 4 cups chicken or vegetable broth
- Salt and pepper to taste
- Fresh cilantro or parsley for garnish

Instructions:

1. In a pot, heat vegetable oil over medium heat.
2. Sauté finely chopped onion until translucent.
3. Add diced lamb or chicken and cook until browned on all sides.
4. Stir in minced garlic, ground cumin, ground coriander, and ground cinnamon. Cook for 1-2 minutes until fragrant.

5. Add chopped tomatoes and cook until they release their juices.
6. Pour in cracked wheat (jareesh) and chicken or vegetable broth.
7. Season with salt and pepper to taste.
8. Bring the mixture to a boil, then reduce heat, cover, and simmer for 40-45 minutes or until the cracked wheat is tender.
9. Check the seasoning and adjust if needed.
10. Serve hot, garnished with fresh cilantro or parsley.

HAREES (WHEAT AND MEAT PORRIDGE)

Servings: 4 servings
Time: 2 hours

Ingredients:

- 1 cup whole wheat grains
- 1 cup chicken, diced
- 1 large onion, finely chopped
- 3 cloves garlic, minced
- 2 tablespoons vegetable oil
- 1/2 teaspoon ground cinnamon
- Salt to taste
- 6 cups chicken broth
- Fresh parsley for garnish

Instructions:

1. Wash the whole wheat grains thoroughly and soak them in water for at least 1 hour.
2. In a pot, heat vegetable oil over medium heat.

3. Sauté finely chopped onion until translucent.
4. Add minced garlic and cook until fragrant.
5. Add diced chicken and brown on all sides.
6. Stir in ground cinnamon and salt.
7. Drain the soaked whole wheat grains and add them to the pot.
8. Pour in chicken broth and bring the mixture to a boil.
9. Reduce heat, cover, and simmer for 1.5 to 2 hours, stirring occasionally, until the wheat and meat are fully cooked and the mixture becomes a thick porridge.
10. Check the seasoning and adjust if needed.
11. Serve hot, garnished with fresh parsley.

MAJBOOS (CHICKEN AND RICE)

Servings: 6 servings
Time: 1.5 hours

Ingredients:

- 2 cups basmati rice, soaked and drained
- 1 whole chicken, cut into pieces
- 2 large onions, thinly sliced
- 3 tomatoes, chopped
- 1/4 cup vegetable oil
- 2 tablespoons clarified butter (ghee)
- 4 cloves garlic, minced
- 1 teaspoon ground coriander
- 1 teaspoon ground cumin
- 1 teaspoon ground cinnamon
- 1 teaspoon ground cardamom
- 1 teaspoon ground turmeric

- 1 teaspoon ground black lime (loomi) or substitute with lime zest
- 2 bay leaves
- 4 cups chicken broth
- Salt and pepper to taste
- Fresh coriander or parsley for garnish

Instructions:

1. In a large pot, heat vegetable oil and clarified butter over medium heat.
2. Sauté thinly sliced onions until golden brown and crispy. Remove half for garnish.
3. Add minced garlic to the pot and cook until fragrant.
4. Add chicken pieces and brown on all sides.
5. Stir in ground coriander, ground cumin, ground cinnamon, ground cardamom, ground turmeric, and ground black lime (loomi).
6. Add chopped tomatoes and cook until they release their juices.
7. Pour in soaked and drained basmati rice, stirring to coat the rice with the spices.
8. Add bay leaves, then pour in chicken broth. Season with salt and pepper to taste.
9. Bring the mixture to a boil, then reduce heat, cover, and simmer for 20-25 minutes or until the rice is cooked and the liquid is absorbed.
10. Allow the Majboos to rest for a few minutes, then fluff the rice with a fork.
11. Serve hot, garnished with the reserved crispy onions and fresh coriander or parsley.

QUZI (ROASTED LAMB WITH RICE)

Servings: 6 servings
Time: 3 hours

Ingredients:

- 2 cups basmati rice, soaked and drained
- 1 whole lamb leg or shoulder
- 2 large onions, finely chopped
- 3 tomatoes, chopped
- 1/2 cup vegetable oil
- 1/4 cup clarified butter (ghee)
- 6 cloves garlic, minced
- 2 teaspoons ground coriander
- 2 teaspoons ground cumin
- 1 teaspoon ground cinnamon
- 1 teaspoon ground cardamom
- 1 teaspoon ground turmeric
- 1 teaspoon ground black lime (loomi) or substitute with lime zest
- 2 bay leaves
- 6 cups lamb or beef broth
- Salt and pepper to taste
- Almonds and raisins for garnish
- Fresh coriander or parsley for garnish

Instructions:

1. Preheat the oven to 350°F (180°C).
2. In a large pot, heat vegetable oil and clarified butter over medium heat.
3. Sauté finely chopped onions until golden brown.
4. Add minced garlic and cook until fragrant.
5. Add the lamb leg or shoulder and brown on all sides.

6. Stir in ground coriander, ground cumin, ground cinnamon, ground cardamom, ground turmeric, and ground black lime (loomi).
7. Add chopped tomatoes and cook until they release their juices.
8. Pour in lamb or beef broth and bring the mixture to a boil.
9. Season with salt and pepper to taste.
10. Transfer the lamb and broth mixture to a roasting pan.
11. Cover with foil and roast in the preheated oven for 2 to 2.5 hours, basting occasionally, until the lamb is tender and falls off the bone.
12. In the last 30 minutes of roasting, add soaked and drained basmati rice to the roasting pan, ensuring it's submerged in the broth.
13. Allow the rice to cook in the lamb broth until tender.
14. Garnish with almonds, raisins, and fresh coriander or parsley.

LUBYA (GREEN BEAN STEW) WITH RICE

Servings: 4 servings
Time: 1 hour

Ingredients:

- 2 cups green beans, ends trimmed and cut into bite-sized pieces
- 1 cup lean lamb or beef, cubed
- 1 large onion, finely chopped
- 2 tomatoes, chopped
- 3 cloves garlic, minced
- 2 tablespoons vegetable oil

- 1 teaspoon ground coriander
- 1 teaspoon ground cumin
- 1/2 teaspoon ground cinnamon
- 1/2 teaspoon ground turmeric
- 1/4 teaspoon cayenne pepper (optional)
- 2 cups chicken or vegetable broth
- Salt and pepper to taste
- Cooked basmati rice for serving
- Fresh cilantro or parsley for garnish

Instructions:

1. In a pot, heat vegetable oil over medium heat.
2. Sauté finely chopped onion until translucent.
3. Add cubed lamb or beef and brown on all sides.
4. Stir in minced garlic, ground coriander, ground cumin, ground cinnamon, ground turmeric, and cayenne pepper (if using). Cook for 1-2 minutes until fragrant.
5. Add chopped tomatoes and cook until they release their juices.
6. Add green beans to the pot and mix well with the other ingredients.
7. Pour in chicken or vegetable broth, ensuring it covers the green beans.
8. Bring the stew to a boil, then reduce heat and simmer for 30-40 minutes or until the green beans are tender.
9. Season with salt and pepper to taste.
10. Serve the Lubya over a bed of cooked basmati rice.
11. Garnish with fresh cilantro or parsley.

VEGETABLE BIRYANI

Servings: 4 servings
Time: 1.5 hours

Ingredients:

For the Rice:

- 2 cups basmati rice, soaked and drained
- 4 cups water
- 1 bay leaf
- 2 green cardamom pods
- 2 cloves
- Salt to taste

For the Vegetables:

- 1 cup mixed vegetables (carrots, peas, green beans), chopped
- 1 large onion, thinly sliced
- 2 tomatoes, chopped
- 3 tablespoons vegetable oil
- 2 teaspoons ginger-garlic paste
- 1 teaspoon ground cumin
- 1 teaspoon ground coriander
- 1/2 teaspoon turmeric powder
- 1/2 teaspoon red chili powder
- Salt to taste

For the Biryani:

- 1/4 cup chopped mint leaves
- 1/4 cup chopped cilantro (coriander leaves)
- 1/2 cup fried onions (for garnish)

- Saffron strands soaked in warm milk (optional, for color and aroma)

Instructions:

Preparing the Rice:

1. In a pot, bring 4 cups of water to a boil.
2. Add soaked and drained basmati rice, bay leaf, green cardamom pods, cloves, and salt.
3. Cook the rice until it's 70-80% cooked. Drain excess water and set aside.

Preparing the Vegetables:

1. In a large pan, heat vegetable oil over medium heat.
2. Sauté thinly sliced onions until golden brown.
3. Add ginger-garlic paste and cook until the raw smell disappears.
4. Add chopped tomatoes and cook until they become soft.
5. Stir in ground cumin, ground coriander, turmeric powder, red chili powder, and salt.
6. Add the mixed vegetables and cook for 5-7 minutes until they are partially cooked.
7. Remove the pan from heat.

Layering the Biryani:

1. Preheat the oven to 350°F (180°C).
2. In a deep ovenproof dish, layer half of the partially cooked rice.
3. Spread the cooked vegetables over the rice layer.
4. Sprinkle chopped mint leaves and cilantro over the vegetables.

5. Layer the remaining rice over the vegetables.
6. Drizzle saffron-infused milk over the rice for color and aroma (optional).
7. Top with fried onions for added crunch and flavor.

Baking the Biryani:

1. Cover the dish tightly with foil.
2. Bake in the preheated oven for 20-25 minutes or until the rice is fully cooked and aromatic.
3. Allow the biryani to rest for a few minutes before serving.

Serving:

1. Gently fluff the biryani with a fork to mix the layers.
2. Serve hot, garnished with additional mint, cilantro, and fried onions.

FISH KABSA

Servings: 4 servings
Time: 1.5 hours

Ingredients:

For the Rice:

- 2 cups basmati rice, soaked and drained
- 4 cups water
- 1 bay leaf
- 2 green cardamom pods
- 2 cloves

- Salt to taste

For the Fish:

- 1 pound white fish fillets (such as cod or tilapia)
- 2 tablespoons vegetable oil
- 1 onion, finely chopped
- 2 tomatoes, chopped
- 3 tablespoons tomato paste
- 1 teaspoon ground cumin
- 1 teaspoon ground coriander
- 1/2 teaspoon ground cinnamon
- 1/2 teaspoon ground turmeric
- 1/2 teaspoon red chili powder
- Salt and pepper to taste
- 2 cups fish or vegetable broth

For the Kabsa Spice Mix:

- 1 teaspoon ground cumin
- 1 teaspoon ground coriander
- 1 teaspoon ground cinnamon
- 1 teaspoon ground cardamom

Instructions:

Preparing the Rice:

1. In a pot, bring 4 cups of water to a boil.
2. Add soaked and drained basmati rice, bay leaf, green cardamom pods, cloves, and salt.
3. Cook the rice until it's 70-80% cooked. Drain excess water and set aside.

Preparing the Fish:

1. In a large pan, heat vegetable oil over medium heat.
2. Sauté finely chopped onion until translucent.
3. Add chopped tomatoes and cook until they become soft.
4. Stir in tomato paste, ground cumin, ground coriander, ground cinnamon, ground turmeric, red chili powder, salt, and pepper.
5. Add fish fillets to the pan and cook for 2-3 minutes on each side until they are lightly browned.
6. Pour in fish or vegetable broth, cover, and simmer for 15-20 minutes or until the fish is cooked through.

Preparing the Kabsa Spice Mix:

1. In a small bowl, mix together ground cumin, ground coriander, ground cinnamon, and ground cardamom.

Layering the Kabsa:

1. Preheat the oven to 350°F (180°C).
2. In an ovenproof dish, layer half of the partially cooked rice.
3. Place the cooked fish and tomato sauce over the rice.
4. Sprinkle the Kabsa spice mix over the fish.
5. Layer the remaining rice over the fish.
6. Drizzle some of the broth from the fish over the top.

Baking the Fish Kabsa:

1. Cover the dish tightly with foil.
2. Bake in the preheated oven for 20-25 minutes or until the rice is fully cooked and infused with the flavors.

3. Allow the Fish Kabsa to rest for a few minutes before serving.

Serving:

1. Gently mix the rice and fish before serving.
2. Serve hot, garnished with fresh herbs or lemon wedges.

MAQLUBA (UPSIDE-DOWN RICE)

Servings: 6 servings
Time: 2 hours

Ingredients:

For the Rice:

- 2 cups basmati rice, soaked and drained
- 4 cups water
- 1 bay leaf
- 2 green cardamom pods
- 2 cloves
- Salt to taste

For the Chicken and Vegetables:

- 1 whole chicken, cut into pieces
- 2 large onions, thinly sliced
- 3 tomatoes, chopped
- 2 cups cauliflower florets
- 2 cups eggplant, cubed
- 1 cup carrots, sliced
- 1/2 cup vegetable oil

- 3 tablespoons tomato paste
- 1 teaspoon ground cumin
- 1 teaspoon ground coriander
- 1/2 teaspoon ground cinnamon
- 1/2 teaspoon ground turmeric
- Salt and pepper to taste
- 6 cups chicken or vegetable broth

Instructions:

Preparing the Rice:

1. In a pot, bring 4 cups of water to a boil.
2. Add soaked and drained basmati rice, bay leaf, green cardamom pods, cloves, and salt.
3. Cook the rice until it's 70-80% cooked. Drain excess water and set aside.

Preparing the Chicken and Vegetables:

1. In a large pan, heat vegetable oil over medium heat.
2. Sauté thinly sliced onions until golden brown.
3. Add chicken pieces and brown on all sides.
4. Stir in chopped tomatoes, tomato paste, ground cumin, ground coriander, ground cinnamon, ground turmeric, salt, and pepper.
5. Add cauliflower florets, eggplant, and carrots to the pan. Mix well.
6. Pour in chicken or vegetable broth, ensuring it covers the chicken and vegetables.
7. Bring the mixture to a boil, then reduce heat and simmer for 30-40 minutes or until the chicken is cooked and the vegetables are tender.

Layering the Maqluba:

1. Preheat the oven to 350°F (180°C).
2. In an ovenproof dish, layer half of the partially cooked rice.
3. Arrange the cooked chicken and vegetables over the rice.
4. Top with the remaining rice.

Baking the Maqluba:

1. Cover the dish tightly with foil.
2. Bake in the preheated oven for 20-25 minutes or until the rice is fully cooked and the flavors meld.
3. Allow the Maqluba to rest for a few minutes before serving.

Serving:

1. Gently mix the layers before serving.
2. Invert the dish onto a serving platter to reveal the beautiful upside-down presentation.
3. Serve hot, garnished with fresh herbs or toasted nuts.

LAMB AND CHICKPEA PILAF

Servings: 4 servings
Time: 1.5 hours

Ingredients:

For the Rice:

- 2 cups basmati rice, soaked and drained

- 4 cups water
- 1 bay leaf
- 2 green cardamom pods
- 2 cloves
- Salt to taste

For the Lamb and Chickpea Mixture:

- 1 pound lamb, cubed
- 1 cup cooked chickpeas (canned or boiled)
- 1 large onion, finely chopped
- 2 tomatoes, chopped
- 3 tablespoons vegetable oil
- 2 tablespoons clarified butter (ghee)
- 3 cloves garlic, minced
- 1 teaspoon ground cumin
- 1 teaspoon ground coriander
- 1/2 teaspoon ground cinnamon
- 1/2 teaspoon ground turmeric
- 1/4 teaspoon cayenne pepper (optional)
- Salt and pepper to taste
- 4 cups lamb or vegetable broth

Instructions:

Preparing the Rice:

1. In a pot, bring 4 cups of water to a boil.
2. Add soaked and drained basmati rice, bay leaf, green cardamom pods, cloves, and salt.
3. Cook the rice until it's 70-80% cooked. Drain excess water and set aside.

Preparing the Lamb and Chickpea Mixture:

1. In a large pan, heat vegetable oil and clarified butter over medium heat.
2. Sauté finely chopped onion until translucent.
3. Add cubed lamb and brown on all sides.
4. Stir in minced garlic, ground cumin, ground coriander, ground cinnamon, ground turmeric, and cayenne pepper (if using). Cook for 1-2 minutes until fragrant.
5. Add chopped tomatoes and cook until they release their juices.
6. Add cooked chickpeas to the pan and mix well.
7. Pour in lamb or vegetable broth, ensuring it covers the lamb and chickpeas.
8. Bring the mixture to a boil, then reduce heat and simmer for 30-40 minutes or until the lamb is tender.

Layering the Pilaf:

1. Preheat the oven to 350°F (180°C).
2. In an ovenproof dish, layer half of the partially cooked rice.
3. Spread the lamb and chickpea mixture over the rice.
4. Top with the remaining rice.

Baking the Pilaf:

1. Cover the dish tightly with foil.
2. Bake in the preheated oven for 20-25 minutes or until the rice is fully cooked and infused with the flavors.
3. Allow the Lamb and Chickpea Pilaf to rest for a few minutes before serving.

Serving:

1. Gently mix the layers before serving.

2. Serve hot, garnished with fresh herbs or toasted nuts.

MEAT AND POULTRY DISHES

CHICKEN MANDI

Servings: 4 servings
Time: 2 hours

Ingredients:

For the Rice:

- 2 cups basmati rice, soaked and drained
- 4 cups water
- 1 bay leaf
- 2 green cardamom pods
- 2 cloves
- Salt to taste

For the Chicken:

- 1 whole chicken, skinless and cut into pieces
- 2 large onions, thinly sliced
- 3 tomatoes, chopped
- 1/2 cup vegetable oil
- 2 tablespoons clarified butter (ghee)
- 3 tablespoons Mandi spice mix (combination of cumin, coriander, cinnamon, cardamom)
- 1 teaspoon ground black lime (loomi) or substitute with lime zest
- Salt and pepper to taste
- 4 cups chicken broth

For the Mandi Spice Mix:

- 1 teaspoon ground cumin
- 1 teaspoon ground coriander
- 1 teaspoon ground cinnamon
- 1 teaspoon ground cardamom

Instructions:

Preparing the Rice:

1. In a pot, bring 4 cups of water to a boil.
2. Add soaked and drained basmati rice, bay leaf, green cardamom pods, cloves, and salt.
3. Cook the rice until it's 70-80% cooked. Drain excess water and set aside.

Preparing the Chicken:

1. In a large pan, heat vegetable oil and clarified butter over medium heat.
2. Sauté thinly sliced onions until golden brown.
3. Add chopped tomatoes and cook until they become soft.
4. Stir in Mandi spice mix, ground black lime (loomi), salt, and pepper.
5. Add chicken pieces to the pan and brown on all sides.
6. Pour in chicken broth, ensuring it covers the chicken.
7. Bring the mixture to a boil, then reduce heat and simmer for 30-40 minutes or until the chicken is cooked through.

Layering the Chicken Mandi:

1. Preheat the oven to 350°F (180°C).
2. In an ovenproof dish, layer half of the partially cooked rice.
3. Arrange the cooked chicken and its broth over the rice.
4. Sprinkle the Mandi spice mix over the chicken.
5. Layer the remaining rice over the chicken.

Baking the Chicken Mandi:

1. Cover the dish tightly with foil.
2. Bake in the preheated oven for 20-25 minutes or until the rice is fully cooked and infused with the flavors.
3. Allow the Chicken Mandi to rest for a few minutes before serving.

Serving:

1. Gently mix the layers before serving.
2. Serve hot, garnished with fresh herbs or toasted nuts.

AL HAREES

Servings: 6 servings
Time: 4-6 hours

Ingredients:

- 2 cups whole wheat grains
- 1 cup short-grain rice
- 1 pound lean lamb or chicken, cut into pieces
- 1 large onion, finely chopped
- 3 cloves garlic, minced
- 2 tablespoons clarified butter (ghee)
- Salt to taste

Instructions:

1. Wash the whole wheat grains and short-grain rice thoroughly.
2. In a large pot, combine the whole wheat grains, rice, and cut pieces of lamb or chicken.
3. Add finely chopped onion, minced garlic, and clarified butter (ghee).
4. Season with salt to taste.
5. Pour in enough water to cover the ingredients, ensuring a soupy consistency.
6. Bring the mixture to a boil over high heat.
7. Once boiling, reduce the heat to low and let it simmer.
8. Cover the pot and let Al Harees cook slowly for 4-6 hours, stirring occasionally. The grains should break down, and the meat should become tender.
9. Check the seasoning and add more salt if needed.

10. Al Harees is ready when it reaches a porridge-like consistency.

Serving:

1. Serve Al Harees hot, spooned into individual bowls.
2. Traditionally, it is enjoyed with a dollop of clarified butter (ghee) on top.
3. Al Harees is often served during special occasions and festive celebrations.

SHAWARMA CHICKEN

Servings: 4 servings
Time: 1 hour

Ingredients:

For the Shawarma Marinade:

- 1 pound boneless, skinless chicken thighs
- 2 tablespoons plain yogurt
- 2 tablespoons olive oil
- 2 cloves garlic, minced
- 1 teaspoon ground cumin
- 1 teaspoon ground coriander
- 1 teaspoon ground paprika
- 1 teaspoon ground turmeric
- 1/2 teaspoon ground cinnamon
- Salt and pepper to taste
- Juice of 1 lemon

For Serving:

- Pita bread or flatbreads
- Sliced tomatoes
- Sliced cucumbers
- Chopped lettuce
- Tahini sauce or garlic sauce

Instructions:

Marinating the Chicken:

1. In a bowl, combine all the ingredients for the Shawarma marinade – yogurt, olive oil, minced garlic, ground cumin, ground coriander, ground paprika, ground turmeric, ground cinnamon, salt, pepper, and lemon juice.
2. Add the boneless, skinless chicken thighs to the marinade, ensuring they are well-coated.
3. Cover the bowl and refrigerate for at least 30 minutes, allowing the chicken to absorb the flavors.

Cooking the Shawarma Chicken:

1. Preheat a grill or grill pan over medium-high heat.
2. Thread the marinated chicken thighs onto skewers or cook them directly on the grill.
3. Grill the chicken for 5-7 minutes on each side or until fully cooked and slightly charred.
4. Remove the chicken from the grill and let it rest for a few minutes.
5. Slice the grilled chicken into thin strips.

Serving:

1. Warm the pita bread or flatbreads.

2. Arrange sliced tomatoes, sliced cucumbers, and chopped lettuce on the bread.
3. Add the sliced Shawarma chicken on top.
4. Drizzle with tahini sauce or garlic sauce.
5. Roll or fold the bread to form a wrap or sandwich.

Note: You can also cook the marinated chicken in a skillet over medium-high heat if a grill is not available.

LAMB KOFTA KEBABS

Servings: 4 servings
Time: 1 hour

Ingredients:

For the Lamb Kofta:

- 1 pound ground lamb
- 1 small onion, finely grated
- 2 cloves garlic, minced
- 2 tablespoons fresh parsley, finely chopped
- 1 teaspoon ground cumin
- 1 teaspoon ground coriander
- 1/2 teaspoon ground paprika
- 1/2 teaspoon ground cinnamon
- Salt and pepper to taste

For Serving:

- Pita bread or flatbreads
- Sliced red onions
- Chopped tomatoes

- Chopped cucumbers
- Tzatziki sauce or yogurt-based sauce

Instructions:

Preparing the Lamb Kofta:

1. In a bowl, combine ground lamb, finely grated onion, minced garlic, chopped fresh parsley, ground cumin, ground coriander, ground paprika, ground cinnamon, salt, and pepper.
2. Mix the ingredients thoroughly until well combined.

Forming the Kofta Kebabs:

1. Take a portion of the lamb mixture and shape it into a cylindrical or oval kebab around a skewer or mold.
2. Repeat the process until all the lamb mixture is used.

Cooking the Kofta Kebabs:

1. Preheat a grill or grill pan over medium-high heat.
2. Grill the lamb kofta kebabs for 5-7 minutes on each side or until fully cooked and slightly charred.
3. Ensure the internal temperature of the kofta reaches at least 160°F (71°C).

Serving:

- Warm the pita bread or flatbreads.
- Remove the lamb kofta from the skewers and place them on the bread.
- Top with sliced red onions, chopped tomatoes, and chopped cucumbers.

- Drizzle with tzatziki sauce or your favorite yogurt-based sauce.
- Roll or fold the bread to form a wrap or sandwich.

Note: You can also cook the lamb kofta in the oven or on a stovetop skillet if a grill is not available.

GRILLED LAMB CHOPS

Servings: 4 servings
Time: 30 minutes

Ingredients:

- 8 lamb chops
- 3 tablespoons olive oil
- 3 cloves garlic, minced
- 1 tablespoon fresh rosemary, chopped
- 1 tablespoon fresh thyme, chopped
- 1 teaspoon ground cumin
- Salt and black pepper to taste
- Lemon wedges for serving

Instructions:

1. In a bowl, mix olive oil, minced garlic, chopped rosemary, chopped thyme, ground cumin, salt, and black pepper to create the marinade.
2. Pat the lamb chops dry with paper towels to remove excess moisture.
3. Coat the lamb chops evenly with the prepared marinade, ensuring each chop is well-covered. Allow them to marinate for at least 15 minutes to let the flavors infuse.

4. Preheat the grill to medium-high heat.
5. Remove the lamb chops from the marinade and let any excess drip off.
6. Place the lamb chops on the preheated grill. Grill for 3-4 minutes on each side for medium-rare, or adjust the cooking time according to your desired doneness.
7. During grilling, baste the lamb chops with any remaining marinade for added flavor.
8. Once the lamb chops reach your preferred level of doneness, remove them from the grill.
9. Allow the lamb chops to rest for a few minutes before serving.
10. Serve the grilled lamb chops with lemon wedges on the side for a burst of citrus freshness.

Note: Cooking times may vary depending on the thickness of the lamb chops and the grill temperature.

STUFFED CAMEL

Servings: Designed for large gatherings
Time: Varies (considerable preparation time)

Ingredients:

For the Camel:

• 1 whole camel, cleaned and prepared (Note: You might need to consult a professional butcher for this task)
• Large quantity of rice
• Various whole spices for marination (cumin, coriander, cinnamon, cloves, etc.)
• Salt and pepper to taste

- Butter or ghee for basting

For the Stuffing:

- A mixture of whole chickens, ducks, and turkeys
- Additional rice
- Assorted nuts (such as almonds and pine nuts)
- Raisins and dried fruits
- A blend of aromatic spices

Instructions:

Preparing the Camel:

1. Clean and marinate the camel with a mixture of whole spices, salt, and pepper. Allow it to marinate for at least 24 hours.
2. Carefully stuff the marinated camel with a generous quantity of rice and the additional stuffing ingredients.
3. Sew up the camel to secure the stuffing and keep the flavors intact.
4. Preheat an outdoor pit or a large grill for slow-roasting.
5. Place the marinated and stuffed camel on the grill, and begin the slow-roasting process.
6. Baste the camel with butter or ghee periodically during the cooking process to ensure moisture and enhance flavor.
7. Slow-cook the camel for an extended period until it reaches a tender and succulent texture.
8. Monitor the temperature and adjust the cooking time based on the camel's size.
9. Once fully cooked, carefully remove the camel from the grill.

10. Allow the camel to rest for a while before serving to ensure the juices redistribute.

Serving:

- Present the Stuffed Camel as a centerpiece for a grand feast.
- Serve the rice and stuffing alongside the camel, ensuring a delightful variety of flavors for the guests.
- This traditional dish is often prepared for special occasions and celebrations, creating a memorable culinary experience.
- Enjoy the unique and extraordinary Stuffed Camel, a symbol of hospitality and festivity in some Middle Eastern cultures.

Note: Preparing a Stuffed Camel is an intricate process that requires specialized knowledge and skills. Ensure that you consult with experienced professionals for both the butchering and cooking aspects.

LAMB AND POTATO STEW

Servings: 6 servings
Time: 2 hours

Ingredients:

For the Stew:

- 2 pounds lamb stew meat, cut into cubes
- 3 tablespoons vegetable oil
- 1 large onion, finely chopped

- 3 cloves garlic, minced
- 2 carrots, peeled and sliced
- 4 potatoes, peeled and diced
- 1 cup green peas (fresh or frozen)
- 4 cups lamb or beef broth
- 1 cup tomato puree
- 2 teaspoons dried rosemary
- 1 teaspoon dried thyme
- Salt and pepper to taste

For Garnish:

- Fresh parsley, chopped

Instructions:

Preparing the Lamb and Potato Stew:

1. In a large pot or Dutch oven, heat vegetable oil over medium-high heat.
2. Add the cubed lamb stew meat and brown on all sides. Remove the lamb from the pot and set it aside.
3. In the same pot, add chopped onions and minced garlic. Sauté until the onions are translucent.
4. Return the browned lamb to the pot.
5. Add sliced carrots, diced potatoes, and green peas to the pot.
6. Pour in lamb or beef broth and tomato puree. Stir to combine.
7. Season the stew with dried rosemary, dried thyme, salt, and pepper.

8. Bring the stew to a boil, then reduce the heat to low. Cover and simmer for 1.5 to 2 hours or until the lamb is tender and the vegetables are cooked through.
9. Adjust the seasoning if necessary.

Serving:

1. Ladle the Lamb and Potato Stew into bowls.
2. Garnish with fresh chopped parsley.
3. Serve the stew hot with crusty bread or over a bed of cooked rice.

CHICKEN KABSA

Servings: 4 servings
Time: 1.5 hours

Ingredients:

For the Chicken:

- 1 whole chicken, cut into pieces
- 3 tablespoons vegetable oil
- 1 large onion, finely chopped
- 3 tomatoes, chopped
- 3 tablespoons tomato paste
- 2 teaspoons ground cumin
- 2 teaspoons ground coriander
- 1 teaspoon ground cinnamon
- 1 teaspoon ground cardamom
- 1 teaspoon ground black lime (loomi) or substitute with lime zest
- Salt and pepper to taste

- 4 cups chicken broth

For the Rice:

- 2 cups basmati rice, soaked and drained
- 4 cups water
- 1 bay leaf
- 2 green cardamom pods
- 2 cloves
- Salt to taste

For Garnish:

- Slivered almonds, toasted
- Fresh parsley, chopped

Instructions:

Preparing the Chicken:

1. In a large pot, heat vegetable oil over medium heat.
2. Sauté finely chopped onion until translucent.
3. Add chopped tomatoes and cook until they become soft.
4. Stir in tomato paste, ground cumin, ground coriander, ground cinnamon, ground cardamom, ground black lime (loomi), salt, and pepper.
5. Add chicken pieces to the pot and brown on all sides.
6. Pour in chicken broth, ensuring it covers the chicken.
7. Bring the mixture to a boil, then reduce heat and simmer for 30-40 minutes or until the chicken is cooked through.

Preparing the Rice:

1. In a separate pot, bring 4 cups of water to a boil.

2. Add soaked and drained basmati rice, bay leaf, green cardamom pods, cloves, and salt.
3. Cook the rice until it's 70-80% cooked. Drain excess water and set aside.

Combining Chicken and Rice:

1. Preheat the oven to 350°F (180°C).
2. In an ovenproof dish, layer half of the partially cooked rice.
3. Arrange the cooked chicken and its broth over the rice.
4. Top with the remaining rice.

Baking the Chicken Kabsa:

1. Cover the dish tightly with foil.
2. Bake in the preheated oven for 20-25 minutes or until the rice is fully cooked and infused with the flavors.
3. Allow the Chicken Kabsa to rest for a few minutes before serving.

Serving:

1. Gently mix the layers before serving.
2. Serve hot, garnished with toasted slivered almonds and chopped fresh parsley.

LAMB TAGINE

Servings: 4 servings
Time: 2 hours

Ingredients:

For the Lamb Marinade:

- 1.5 pounds lamb shoulder, cut into cubes
- 2 tablespoons olive oil
- 1 teaspoon ground cumin
- 1 teaspoon ground coriander
- 1 teaspoon ground cinnamon
- 1 teaspoon paprika
- Salt and black pepper to taste

For the Tagine:

- 1 large onion, finely chopped
- 3 cloves garlic, minced
- 2 tablespoons tomato paste
- 1 can (14 oz) diced tomatoes
- 1 cup beef or lamb broth
- 1 cup dried apricots, halved
- 1/2 cup whole blanched almonds
- 2 tablespoons honey
- 1 cinnamon stick
- 2 bay leaves
- Fresh cilantro, chopped (for garnish)

Instructions:

Marinating the Lamb:

- In a bowl, combine olive oil, ground cumin, ground coriander, ground cinnamon, paprika, salt, and black pepper.
- Add the lamb cubes to the marinade, ensuring they are well-coated. Allow them to marinate for at least 30 minutes or refrigerate overnight for enhanced flavor.

Cooking the Lamb:

1. In a tagine or a heavy-bottomed pot, heat olive oil over medium heat.
2. Add finely chopped onion and sauté until translucent.
3. Add minced garlic and continue to sauté for another minute.
4. Add the marinated lamb to the pot and brown on all sides.
5. Stir in tomato paste and cook for 2-3 minutes until it's well incorporated.
6. Pour in the diced tomatoes and beef or lamb broth. Bring the mixture to a simmer.
7. Add dried apricots, whole blanched almonds, honey, cinnamon stick, and bay leaves. Stir to combine.
8. Cover the tagine or pot and simmer on low heat for 1.5 to 2 hours, or until the lamb is tender and the flavors meld.

Serving:

1. Remove the cinnamon stick and bay leaves from the tagine.
2. Serve the Lamb Tagine hot over a bed of couscous or steamed rice.
3. Garnish with chopped fresh cilantro.

BEEF HAREES

Servings: 6 servings
Time: 4-6 hours

Ingredients:

For the Harees:

7. 2 cups whole wheat grains
8. 1 cup short-grain rice
9. 1 pound lean beef, cut into pieces
10. 1 large onion, finely chopped
11. 3 cloves garlic, minced
12. 2 tablespoons clarified butter (ghee)
13. Salt to taste

Instructions:

1. Wash the whole wheat grains and short-grain rice thoroughly.
2. In a large pot, combine the whole wheat grains, rice, and cut pieces of beef.
3. Add finely chopped onion, minced garlic, and clarified butter (ghee).
4. Season with salt to taste.
5. Pour in enough water to cover the ingredients, ensuring a soupy consistency.
6. Bring the mixture to a boil over high heat.
7. Once boiling, reduce the heat to low and let it simmer.
8. Cover the pot and let Beef Harees cook slowly for 4-6 hours, stirring occasionally. The grains should break down, and the beef should become tender.
9. Check the seasoning and add more salt if needed.
10. Beef Harees is ready when it reaches a porridge-like consistency.

Serving:

1. Serve Beef Harees hot, spooned into individual bowls.

2. Traditionally, it is enjoyed with a dollop of clarified butter (ghee) on top.
3. Beef Harees is often served during special occasions and festive celebrations.

SEAFOOD DELIGHTS

GRILLED FISH WITH SPICES

Servings: 4 servings
Time: 30 minutes

Ingredients:

For the Fish:

- 4 fish fillets (such as sea bass or snapper), about 6 ounces each
- 3 tablespoons olive oil
- 2 cloves garlic, minced
- 1 teaspoon ground cumin
- 1 teaspoon ground coriander
- 1 teaspoon paprika

- 1/2 teaspoon ground turmeric
- Salt and black pepper to taste
- Lemon wedges for serving

For Garnish:

- Fresh parsley, chopped

Instructions:

1. Preheat the grill to medium-high heat.
2. In a small bowl, mix olive oil, minced garlic, ground cumin, ground coriander, paprika, ground turmeric, salt, and black pepper to create the spice marinade.
3. Pat the fish fillets dry with paper towels.
4. Brush the fish fillets on both sides with the spice marinade, ensuring they are well-coated.
5. Place the fish fillets on the preheated grill. Grill for approximately 3-4 minutes on each side, or until the fish is cooked through and has grill marks.
6. While grilling, baste the fish with any remaining spice marinade for added flavor.
7. Once the fish is fully cooked, remove it from the grill.
8. Sprinkle the grilled fish with chopped fresh parsley for a burst of freshness.
9. Serve the Grilled Fish with Spices hot, accompanied by lemon wedges on the side.

SHRIMP BIRYANI

Servings: 4 servings
Time: 1.5 hours

Ingredients:

For the Shrimp Marinade:

- 1 pound large shrimp, peeled and deveined
- 1 cup plain yogurt
- 2 tablespoons ginger-garlic paste
- 1 teaspoon ground turmeric
- 1 teaspoon red chili powder
- Salt to taste

For the Biryani:

- 2 cups basmati rice, soaked and drained
- 4 cups water
- 2 tablespoons ghee or vegetable oil
- 1 large onion, thinly sliced
- 2 tomatoes, chopped
- 1/2 cup mint leaves, chopped
- 1/2 cup cilantro (coriander leaves), chopped
- 2 teaspoons biryani masala
- 1 teaspoon ground cumin
- 1 teaspoon ground coriander
- 1/2 teaspoon ground cinnamon
- 4 green cardamom pods
- 4 cloves
- 1 bay leaf
- Salt to taste

For Garnish:

- Fried onions (optional)
- Cashews or almonds, toasted
- Fresh cilantro and mint leaves

Instructions:

Marinating the Shrimp:

1. In a bowl, combine shrimp, yogurt, ginger-garlic paste, ground turmeric, red chili powder, and salt. Mix well, ensuring the shrimp is evenly coated. Allow it to marinate for at least 30 minutes.

Preparing the Rice:

1. In a pot, bring 4 cups of water to a boil.
2. Add soaked and drained basmati rice, a pinch of salt, and cook until it's 70-80% cooked. Drain excess water and set aside.

Cooking the Biryani:

1. In a large pan or pot, heat ghee or vegetable oil over medium heat.
2. Add thinly sliced onions and sauté until golden brown.
3. Add chopped tomatoes, biryani masala, ground cumin, ground coriander, ground cinnamon, green cardamom pods, cloves, bay leaf, and salt. Cook until the tomatoes are soft and the spices are fragrant.
4. Add marinated shrimp to the pot and cook until they are almost fully cooked.

Layering the Biryani:

1. Preheat the oven to 350°F (180°C).
2. In an ovenproof dish, layer half of the partially cooked rice over the shrimp mixture.
3. Sprinkle chopped mint leaves and cilantro over the rice.

4. Add the remaining rice on top.

Baking the Shrimp Biryani:

1. Cover the dish tightly with foil.
2. Bake in the preheated oven for 20-25 minutes or until the rice is fully cooked and the flavors meld.

Serving:

1. Gently mix the layers before serving.
2. Garnish with fried onions (if using), toasted cashews or almonds, and fresh cilantro and mint leaves.
3. Serve the Shrimp Biryani hot, accompanied by raita or a side salad.

FISH KOFTA CURRY

Servings: 4 servings
Time: 1.5 hours

Ingredients:

For the Fish Kofta:

- 1 pound white fish fillets (such as cod or tilapia), chopped
- 1/2 cup onion, finely chopped
- 2 tablespoons fresh cilantro (coriander leaves), chopped
- 1 teaspoon ginger-garlic paste
- 1/2 teaspoon red chili powder
- 1/2 teaspoon ground cumin
- 1/2 teaspoon ground coriander

- 1/4 teaspoon turmeric powder
- Salt to taste
- 1 egg, beaten (for binding)
- Vegetable oil for frying

For the Curry:

- 2 tablespoons vegetable oil
- 1 large onion, finely chopped
- 2 tomatoes, blended into a puree
- 1 teaspoon ginger-garlic paste
- 1 teaspoon ground cumin
- 1 teaspoon ground coriander
- 1/2 teaspoon turmeric powder
- 1/2 teaspoon red chili powder
- 1/2 teaspoon garam masala
- Salt to taste
- 1 cup coconut milk
- Fresh cilantro (coriander leaves) for garnish

Instructions:

Making the Fish Kofta:

1. In a food processor, combine chopped fish fillets, finely chopped onion, chopped cilantro, ginger-garlic paste, red chili powder, ground cumin, ground coriander, turmeric powder, and salt. Blend until you have a smooth mixture.
2. Transfer the fish mixture to a bowl and add the beaten egg. Mix well to form a dough-like consistency.
3. Shape the mixture into small balls to create fish koftas.

4. Heat vegetable oil in a pan over medium-high heat. Fry the fish koftas until golden brown on all sides. Remove and set aside.

Preparing the Curry:

1. In the same pan, add more oil if needed. Sauté finely chopped onion until translucent.
2. Add ginger-garlic paste and cook for a minute until the raw aroma disappears.
3. Stir in ground cumin, ground coriander, turmeric powder, red chili powder, and garam masala. Cook for another minute.
4. Pour in the blended tomato puree and cook until the oil begins to separate from the masala.
5. Add salt to taste and coconut milk. Mix well and let it simmer for a few minutes.
6. Gently place the fried fish koftas into the curry, ensuring they are fully submerged.
7. Simmer for an additional 10-15 minutes, allowing the koftas to absorb the flavors of the curry.

Serving:

1. Garnish the Fish Kofta Curry with fresh cilantro (coriander leaves).
2. Serve hot over steamed rice or with naan for a delightful meal.

SPICY FISH STEW

Servings: 4 servings
Time: 45 minutes

Ingredients:

- 1 pound white fish fillets (such as cod or tilapia), cut into chunks
- 2 tablespoons vegetable oil
- 1 large onion, finely chopped
- 3 cloves garlic, minced
- 1 teaspoon ginger, grated
- 1 teaspoon ground cumin
- 1 teaspoon ground coriander
- 1 teaspoon paprika
- 1/2 teaspoon red chili powder (adjust to taste)
- 1/2 teaspoon turmeric powder
- 1 can (14 oz) diced tomatoes
- 1 cup fish or vegetable broth
- 1 bell pepper, thinly sliced
- 1 zucchini, sliced
- Salt and black pepper to taste
- Fresh cilantro (coriander leaves) for garnish
- Lemon wedges for serving

Instructions:

1. In a large pot, heat vegetable oil over medium heat.
2. Add finely chopped onion and sauté until translucent.
3. Add minced garlic and grated ginger. Sauté for another minute until fragrant.
4. Stir in ground cumin, ground coriander, paprika, red chili powder, and turmeric powder. Mix well to coat the onions with the spices.
5. Add diced tomatoes (with their juices) and fish or vegetable broth. Bring the mixture to a simmer.

6. Gently add fish chunks to the pot and cook for 5-7 minutes or until the fish is almost cooked through.
7. Add sliced bell pepper and zucchini to the stew. Simmer for an additional 5-7 minutes until the vegetables are tender.
8. Season the stew with salt and black pepper to taste.
9. Garnish with fresh cilantro (coriander leaves).

Serving:

1. Serve the Spicy Fish Stew hot, ladled into bowls.
2. Squeeze fresh lemon juice over the stew before serving for a burst of citrusy freshness.

SEAFOOD MACHBOOS

Servings: 4 servings
Time: 1.5 hours

Ingredients:

For the Seafood Marinade:

- 1 pound mixed seafood (shrimp, fish, calamari), cleaned and deveined
- 2 tablespoons vegetable oil
- 1 teaspoon ground coriander
- 1 teaspoon ground cumin
- 1 teaspoon ground cinnamon
- 1/2 teaspoon ground turmeric
- 1/2 teaspoon red chili powder
- Salt and black pepper to taste
- Juice of 1 lemon

For the Machboos:

- 2 cups basmati rice, soaked and drained
- 4 cups water
- 2 tablespoons vegetable oil
- 1 large onion, finely chopped
- 3 tomatoes, blended into a puree
- 2 tablespoons tomato paste
- 1 teaspoon ginger-garlic paste
- 1 teaspoon ground coriander
- 1 teaspoon ground cumin
- 1/2 teaspoon ground cinnamon
- 1/2 teaspoon ground cardamom
- 1/2 teaspoon ground cloves
- 1/2 teaspoon ground nutmeg
- 1/2 teaspoon ground black lime (loomi) or substitute with lime zest
- Salt to taste
- 4 cups fish or vegetable broth
- Fresh cilantro and mint leaves for garnish

Instructions:

Marinating the Seafood:

1. In a bowl, combine cleaned and deveined seafood with vegetable oil, ground coriander, ground cumin, ground cinnamon, ground turmeric, red chili powder, salt, black pepper, and lemon juice. Mix well and let it marinate for at least 30 minutes.

Preparing the Rice:

1. In a pot, bring 4 cups of water to a boil.

2. Add soaked and drained basmati rice, a pinch of salt, and cook until it's 70-80% cooked. Drain excess water and set aside.

Making the Machboos:

1. In a large pot, heat vegetable oil over medium heat.
2. Add finely chopped onion and sauté until translucent.
3. Stir in ginger-garlic paste and cook for a minute until the raw aroma disappears.
4. Add tomato puree, tomato paste, ground coriander, ground cumin, ground cinnamon, ground cardamom, ground cloves, ground nutmeg, ground black lime (loomi) or lime zest, and salt. Cook until the oil begins to separate from the masala.
5. Add marinated seafood to the pot and cook until the seafood is almost fully cooked.
6. Pour in fish or vegetable broth. Mix well and let it simmer for a few minutes.

Layering and Cooking the Machboos:

1. Preheat the oven to 350°F (180°C).
2. In an ovenproof dish, layer half of the partially cooked rice over the seafood mixture.
3. Pour the remaining seafood and broth over the rice.
4. Top with the remaining rice.

Baking the Seafood Machboos:

1. Cover the dish tightly with foil.
2. Bake in the preheated oven for 20-25 minutes or until the rice is fully cooked and infused with the flavors.

Serving:

1. Gently mix the layers before serving.
2. Garnish with fresh cilantro and mint leaves.
3. Serve the Seafood Machboos hot, accompanied by a side salad or yogurt raita.

EMIRATI STYLE PRAWN MASALA

Servings: 4 servings
Time: 40 minutes

Ingredients:

For the Prawn Marinade:

- 1 pound large prawns, peeled and deveined
- 1 tablespoon vegetable oil
- 1 teaspoon red chili powder
- 1/2 teaspoon ground turmeric
- 1/2 teaspoon ground coriander
- Salt to taste

For the Masala:

- 2 tablespoons vegetable oil
- 1 large onion, finely chopped
- 2 tomatoes, blended into a puree
- 1 teaspoon ginger-garlic paste
- 1 teaspoon ground cumin
- 1 teaspoon ground coriander
- 1/2 teaspoon ground fennel seeds
- 1/2 teaspoon garam masala

- 1/2 teaspoon ground black lime (loomi) or substitute with lime zest
- Salt to taste
- Fresh cilantro (coriander leaves) for garnish

Instructions:

Marinating the Prawns:

1. In a bowl, combine peeled and deveined prawns with vegetable oil, red chili powder, ground turmeric, ground coriander, and salt. Mix well and let it marinate for at least 15 minutes.

Making the Masala:

1. In a pan, heat vegetable oil over medium heat.
2. Add finely chopped onion and sauté until translucent.
3. Stir in ginger-garlic paste and cook for a minute until the raw aroma disappears.
4. Add ground cumin, ground coriander, ground fennel seeds, garam masala, ground black lime (loomi) or lime zest, and salt. Mix well.
5. Pour in the blended tomato puree and cook until the oil begins to separate from the masala.
6. Add the marinated prawns to the pan and cook until they are fully cooked and coated with the masala.
7. Adjust the seasoning if needed.

Serving:

1. Garnish the Emirati Style Prawn Masala with fresh cilantro (coriander leaves).

2. Serve hot over steamed rice or with traditional Emirati bread.

FISH HAREES

Servings: 4 servings
Time: 2 hours

Ingredients:

For the Fish:

- 1 pound white fish fillets (such as cod or tilapia), cut into chunks
- 2 tablespoons vegetable oil
- 1 large onion, finely chopped
- 3 cloves garlic, minced
- 1 teaspoon ground cumin
- 1 teaspoon ground coriander
- 1/2 teaspoon ground turmeric
- 1/2 teaspoon ground cinnamon
- Salt and black pepper to taste

For the Harees:

- 1 cup whole wheat grains
- 1/2 cup short-grain rice
- 1 pound fish bones or heads (for broth)
- 1 large onion, finely chopped
- 3 cloves garlic, minced
- 2 tablespoons clarified butter (ghee)
- Salt to taste

Instructions:

Preparing the Fish:

1. In a pan, heat vegetable oil over medium heat.
2. Add finely chopped onion and sauté until translucent.
3. Stir in minced garlic, ground cumin, ground coriander, ground turmeric, ground cinnamon, salt, and black pepper. Cook for a minute until the spices are fragrant.
4. Add fish chunks to the pan and cook until they are fully cooked. Set aside.

Preparing the Harees:

1. Wash whole wheat grains and short-grain rice thoroughly.
2. In a large pot, combine whole wheat grains, rice, fish bones or heads, finely chopped onion, minced garlic, and clarified butter (ghee).
3. Season with salt and add enough water to cover the ingredients, ensuring a soupy consistency.
4. Bring the mixture to a boil over high heat.
5. Once boiling, reduce the heat to low and let it simmer.
6. Cover the pot and let Fish Harees cook slowly for 2 hours, stirring occasionally. The grains should break down, and the fish bones should infuse the broth.
7. Check the seasoning and add more salt if needed.

Serving:

1. Remove fish bones or heads from the Harees.
2. Serve Fish Harees hot, spooned into individual bowls.
3. Optionally, drizzle with extra clarified butter (ghee) before serving.

LEMON BUTTER GARLIC PRAWNS

Servings: 4 servings
Time: 20 minutes

Ingredients:

- 1 pound large prawns, peeled and deveined
- 3 tablespoons unsalted butter
- 3 tablespoons olive oil
- 6 cloves garlic, minced
- Zest of 1 lemon
- Juice of 1 lemon
- 1 teaspoon red pepper flakes (optional, for heat)
- Salt and black pepper to taste
- Fresh parsley, chopped (for garnish)

Instructions:

1. In a large skillet, heat butter and olive oil over medium heat until the butter is melted.
2. Add minced garlic to the skillet and sauté for 1-2 minutes until it becomes fragrant.
3. Add the peeled and deveined prawns to the skillet. Cook for 2-3 minutes on each side or until they turn pink and opaque.
4. Season the prawns with salt, black pepper, and red pepper flakes (if using). Stir well to coat the prawns evenly.
5. Add lemon zest and lemon juice to the skillet. Stir to combine and let it simmer for an additional 1-2 minutes.
6. Taste and adjust the seasoning if needed.
7. Remove the skillet from heat.

Serving:

1. Transfer the Lemon Butter Garlic Prawns to a serving platter.
2. Garnish with chopped fresh parsley.
3. Serve hot over a bed of steamed rice or with crusty bread to soak up the delicious sauce.

SPICED CRAB CURRY

Servings: 4 servings
Time: 45 minutes

Ingredients:

For the Crab Marinade:

- 2 pounds whole crabs, cleaned and cracked
- 2 tablespoons vegetable oil
- 1 teaspoon red chili powder
- 1 teaspoon ground turmeric
- Salt to taste

For the Curry:

- 2 tablespoons vegetable oil
- 1 large onion, finely chopped
- 3 tomatoes, blended into a puree
- 1 teaspoon ginger-garlic paste
- 1 teaspoon ground cumin
- 1 teaspoon ground coriander
- 1/2 teaspoon red chili powder (adjust to taste)
- 1/2 teaspoon ground fennel seeds

- 1/2 teaspoon ground mustard seeds
- 1/2 teaspoon ground black lime (loomi) or substitute with lime zest
- Salt to taste
- 1 cup coconut milk
- Fresh cilantro (coriander leaves) for garnish

Instructions:

Marinating the Crab:

1. In a bowl, combine cleaned and cracked crabs with vegetable oil, red chili powder, ground turmeric, and salt. Mix well and let them marinate for at least 15 minutes.

Making the Curry:

1. In a large pan, heat vegetable oil over medium heat.
2. Add finely chopped onion and sauté until translucent.
3. Stir in ginger-garlic paste and cook for a minute until the raw aroma disappears.
4. Add ground cumin, ground coriander, red chili powder, ground fennel seeds, ground mustard seeds, ground black lime (loomi) or lime zest, and salt. Mix well.
5. Pour in the blended tomato puree and cook until the oil begins to separate from the masala.
6. Add the marinated crabs to the pan and coat them with the masala. Cook for 5-7 minutes.
7. Pour in coconut milk and mix well. Let it simmer for an additional 10-15 minutes until the crabs are fully cooked and the flavors meld.

Serving:

1. Garnish the Spiced Crab Curry with fresh cilantro (coriander leaves).
2. Serve hot over steamed rice or with traditional bread.

GRILLED LOBSTER WITH HERBS

Servings: 2 servings
Time: 30 minutes

Ingredients:

- 2 whole lobsters, split in half
- 1/4 cup olive oil
- 2 tablespoons fresh lemon juice
- 3 cloves garlic, minced
- 1 tablespoon fresh parsley, chopped
- 1 tablespoon fresh cilantro (coriander leaves), chopped
- 1 teaspoon fresh thyme leaves
- Salt and black pepper to taste
- Lemon wedges for serving

Instructions:

1. Preheat the grill to medium-high heat.
2. In a bowl, whisk together olive oil, lemon juice, minced garlic, chopped parsley, chopped cilantro, and fresh thyme leaves. Season with salt and black pepper.
3. Place the lobster halves on a cutting board, shell side down. Use a sharp knife to split each lobster in half.
4. Brush the lobster halves generously with the herb-infused olive oil mixture, ensuring they are well-coated.
5. Place the lobster halves on the preheated grill, shell side down. Grill for 4-5 minutes until the shells start to char.

6. Flip the lobster halves and continue grilling for an additional 4-5 minutes, or until the lobster meat is opaque and cooked through.
7. While grilling, baste the lobster halves with any remaining herb-infused olive oil for added flavor.
8. Remove the grilled lobster halves from the grill and transfer them to a serving platter.

Serving:

1. Drizzle any remaining herb-infused olive oil over the grilled lobster.
2. Serve hot with lemon wedges on the side for squeezing over the lobster.

BREAD AND PASTRIES

KHAMEER BREAD

Servings: 6 pieces
Time: 2 hours (including rising time)

Ingredients:

- 2 1/2 cups all-purpose flour
- 1 tablespoon sugar
- 1 teaspoon salt
- 1 teaspoon active dry yeast
- 1 cup warm milk
- 2 tablespoons vegetable oil
- Sesame seeds for sprinkling (optional)

Instructions:

1. In a small bowl, combine warm milk and sugar. Stir until the sugar is dissolved. Sprinkle the active dry yeast over the mixture and let it sit for 5-10 minutes, or until frothy.
2. In a large mixing bowl, combine all-purpose flour and salt.
3. Make a well in the center of the flour mixture and pour in the yeast mixture and vegetable oil.
4. Mix the ingredients until a dough forms. Knead the dough on a floured surface for about 8-10 minutes, or until it becomes smooth and elastic.
5. Place the dough in a greased bowl, cover it with a damp cloth, and let it rise in a warm place for 1 hour, or until it doubles in size.
6. Preheat the oven to 375°F (190°C).
7. Punch down the risen dough and divide it into 6 equal portions.
8. Roll each portion into a ball and flatten it into a round disc (about 6 inches in diameter).
9. Place the flattened dough discs on a baking sheet, leaving some space between each.
10. If desired, sprinkle sesame seeds on top of each Khameer bread.
11. Bake in the preheated oven for 12-15 minutes, or until the bread is golden brown and cooked through.
12. Serve Khameer Bread warm, either on its own or paired with your favorite spreads.

RGHAIF (LAYERED FLATBREAD)

Servings: 8 pieces
Time: 2 hours (including rising time)

Ingredients:

For the Dough:

- 3 cups all-purpose flour
- 1 teaspoon salt
- 1 teaspoon sugar
- 1 tablespoon active dry yeast
- 1 1/4 cups warm water
- 2 tablespoons vegetable oil

For Layering:

- 1 cup unsalted butter, melted
- 1/2 cup vegetable oil

Instructions:

Preparing the Dough:

1. In a small bowl, combine warm water, sugar, and active dry yeast. Allow it to sit for 5-10 minutes, or until the mixture becomes frothy.
2. In a large mixing bowl, combine all-purpose flour and salt.
3. Make a well in the center of the flour mixture and pour in the yeast mixture and vegetable oil.
4. Mix the ingredients until a dough forms. Knead the dough on a floured surface for about 8-10 minutes, or until it becomes smooth and elastic.
5. Place the dough in a greased bowl, cover it with a damp cloth, and let it rise in a warm place for 1 hour, or until it doubles in size.

Assembling Rghaif:

1. Preheat the oven to 375°F (190°C).
2. Punch down the risen dough and divide it into 8 equal portions.
3. Roll each portion into a ball and let them rest for 10 minutes.
4. In a small bowl, mix melted butter and vegetable oil.
5. Take one ball of dough and roll it out into a thin circle on a floured surface.
6. Brush the circle with the butter and oil mixture.
7. Place another circle of dough on top and brush it with the mixture.
8. Repeat the process, stacking the circles on top of each other with butter and oil between each layer.
9. Roll out the layered circles into a larger circle.
10. Transfer the layered dough to a baking sheet.

Baking Rghaif:

1. Bake in the preheated oven for 20-25 minutes, or until the Rghaif is golden brown and cooked through.
2. Remove from the oven and let it cool slightly.
3. Slice into wedges and serve warm.

MANAKISH (HERBED FLATBREAD)

Servings: 4 pieces
Time: 1.5 hours (including rising time)

Ingredients:

For the Dough:

- 2 1/2 cups all-purpose flour
- 1 teaspoon sugar
- 1 teaspoon salt
- 1 tablespoon active dry yeast
- 1 cup warm water
- 2 tablespoons olive oil

For the Topping:

- 1/4 cup olive oil
- 1 cup za'atar spice mix
- 1 small red onion, finely diced (optional)

Instructions:

Preparing the Dough:

1. In a small bowl, combine warm water, sugar, and active dry yeast. Allow it to sit for 5-10 minutes, or until the mixture becomes frothy.
2. In a large mixing bowl, combine all-purpose flour and salt.
3. Make a well in the center of the flour mixture and pour in the yeast mixture and olive oil.
4. Mix the ingredients until a dough forms. Knead the dough on a floured surface for about 8-10 minutes, or until it becomes smooth and elastic.
5. Place the dough in a greased bowl, cover it with a damp cloth, and let it rise in a warm place for 1 hour, or until it doubles in size.

Assembling Manakish:

1. Preheat the oven to 425°F (220°C).

2. Punch down the risen dough and divide it into 4 equal portions.
3. Roll each portion into a ball and let them rest for 10 minutes.
4. On a floured surface, roll out each ball into a thin circle.

For the Topping:

1. Mix olive oil and za'atar spice mix in a bowl to create a paste.

Baking Manakish:

1. Place the rolled-out dough circles on a baking sheet.
2. Spread the za'atar and olive oil mixture evenly over each dough circle.
3. If desired, sprinkle finely diced red onion on top.
4. Bake in the preheated oven for 12-15 minutes, or until the edges are golden brown.
5. Slice into wedges and serve warm.

ARABIC BREAD ROLLS

Servings: 12 rolls
Time: 2 hours (including rising time)

Ingredients:

For the Dough:

- 4 cups all-purpose flour
- 1 tablespoon sugar
- 1 teaspoon salt

- 1 tablespoon active dry yeast
- 1 1/2 cups warm water
- 3 tablespoons olive oil

For Brushing:

- 2 tablespoons olive oil

Instructions:

Preparing the Dough:

1. In a small bowl, combine warm water, sugar, and active dry yeast. Allow it to sit for 5-10 minutes, or until the mixture becomes frothy.
2. In a large mixing bowl, combine all-purpose flour and salt.
3. Make a well in the center of the flour mixture and pour in the yeast mixture and olive oil.
4. Mix the ingredients until a dough forms. Knead the dough on a floured surface for about 8-10 minutes, or until it becomes smooth and elastic.
5. Place the dough in a greased bowl, cover it with a damp cloth, and let it rise in a warm place for 1 hour, or until it doubles in size.

Shaping the Rolls:

1. Preheat the oven to 400°F (200°C).
2. Punch down the risen dough and divide it into 12 equal portions.
3. Roll each portion into a ball and place them on a baking sheet lined with parchment paper.
4. Brush the tops of the rolls with olive oil.

5. Cover the rolls with a clean cloth and let them rise for an additional 30 minutes.

Baking Arabic Bread Rolls:

1. Bake in the preheated oven for 15-18 minutes, or until the rolls are golden brown.
2. Remove from the oven and let the rolls cool on a wire rack.
3. Enjoy these soft and pillowy rolls as a perfect accompaniment to your favorite dips, soups, or grilled dishes.

CHEESE SAMBOUSEK

Servings: 20 sambousek
Time: 1.5 hours

Ingredients:

For the Dough:

- 3 cups all-purpose flour
- 1 cup unsalted butter, melted
- 1 cup plain yogurt
- 1 teaspoon baking powder
- 1/2 teaspoon salt

For the Cheese Filling:

- 2 cups feta cheese, crumbled
- 1 cup mozzarella cheese, shredded
- 1/2 cup fresh parsley, finely chopped

- 1/2 teaspoon black pepper
- 1 egg, beaten (for egg wash)

Instructions:

Preparing the Dough:

1. In a large bowl, combine all-purpose flour, melted butter, plain yogurt, baking powder, and salt. Mix until a soft dough forms.
2. Cover the bowl with a damp cloth and let the dough rest for 30 minutes.

Making the Cheese Filling:

1. In a separate bowl, mix crumbled feta cheese, shredded mozzarella cheese, chopped fresh parsley, and black pepper. Combine well.

Shaping the Cheese Sambousek:

1. Preheat the oven to 375°F (190°C).
2. Take a small portion of the dough and roll it into a ball (about the size of a walnut).
3. On a floured surface, roll out the dough ball into a small circle.
4. Place a spoonful of the cheese filling in the center of the circle.
5. Fold the edges of the dough over the filling, forming a half-moon shape. Press the edges to seal.
6. Place the filled sambousek on a baking sheet lined with parchment paper.
7. Repeat the process with the remaining dough and filling.

Baking Cheese Sambousek:

1. Brush the tops of the sambousek with beaten egg for a golden finish.
2. Bake in the preheated oven for 15-20 minutes, or until the sambousek are golden brown and cooked through.
3. Remove from the oven and let them cool slightly before serving.
4. Enjoy these delightful cheese-filled pastries as an appetizer or snack, perfect for sharing with family and friends!

KAAK BREAD

Servings: 10 pieces
Time: 2 hours (including rising time)

Ingredients:

For the Dough:

- 3 cups all-purpose flour
- 1 tablespoon sugar
- 1 teaspoon salt
- 1 tablespoon active dry yeast
- 1 cup warm water
- 1/4 cup olive oil

For the Topping:

- 1/2 cup sesame seeds

Instructions:

Preparing the Dough:

1. In a small bowl, combine warm water, sugar, and active dry yeast. Allow it to sit for 5-10 minutes, or until the mixture becomes frothy.
2. In a large mixing bowl, combine all-purpose flour and salt.
3. Make a well in the center of the flour mixture and pour in the yeast mixture and olive oil.
4. Mix the ingredients until a dough forms. Knead the dough on a floured surface for about 8-10 minutes, or until it becomes smooth and elastic.
5. Place the dough in a greased bowl, cover it with a damp cloth, and let it rise in a warm place for 1 hour, or until it doubles in size.

Shaping Kaak Bread:

1. Preheat the oven to 400°F (200°C).
2. Punch down the risen dough and divide it into 10 equal portions.
3. Roll each portion into a rope shape, about 8 inches long.
4. Join the ends of each rope to form a circle, pinching the ends to seal.
5. Place the shaped Kaak bread on a baking sheet lined with parchment paper.

Topping Kaak Bread:

1. Dip each Kaak circle into water, then into sesame seeds, ensuring they stick to the surface.

Baking Kaak Bread:

1. Bake in the preheated oven for 15-18 minutes, or until the Kaak is golden brown.
2. Remove from the oven and let the Kaak cool on a wire rack.
3. Enjoy the delightful crunch and nutty flavor of Kaak bread as a snack or with your favorite dips and spreads!

EMIRATI PITA BREAD

Servings: 8 pitas
Time: 2 hours (including rising time)

Ingredients:

For the Dough:

- 3 cups all-purpose flour
- 1 teaspoon sugar
- 1 teaspoon salt
- 1 tablespoon active dry yeast
- 1 1/4 cups warm water
- 2 tablespoons olive oil

For Brushing:

- Olive oil for brushing

Instructions:

Preparing the Dough:

1. In a small bowl, combine warm water, sugar, and active dry yeast. Allow it to sit for 5-10 minutes, or until the mixture becomes frothy.
2. In a large mixing bowl, combine all-purpose flour and salt.
3. Make a well in the center of the flour mixture and pour in the yeast mixture and olive oil.
4. Mix the ingredients until a dough forms. Knead the dough on a floured surface for about 8-10 minutes, or until it becomes smooth and elastic.
5. Place the dough in a greased bowl, cover it with a damp cloth, and let it rise in a warm place for 1 hour, or until it doubles in size.

Shaping Emirati Pita Bread:

1. Preheat the oven to 475°F (245°C).
2. Punch down the risen dough and divide it into 8 equal portions.
3. Roll each portion into a ball and let them rest for 10 minutes.
4. On a floured surface, roll out each ball into a round disc (about 6-8 inches in diameter).

Baking Emirati Pita Bread:

1. Place the rolled-out dough discs on a baking sheet.
2. Brush the tops of the discs lightly with olive oil.
3. Bake in the preheated oven for 8-10 minutes, or until the pita bread puffs up and the edges are golden brown.
4. Remove from the oven and let the pita bread cool on a wire rack.

5. Enjoy the soft and pillowy texture of these homemade pitas, perfect for stuffing with your favorite fillings or as an accompaniment to dips and salads!

ZAATAR BREADSTICKS

Servings: 16 breadsticks
Time: 2 hours (including rising time)

Ingredients:

For the Dough:

- 2 1/2 cups all-purpose flour
- 1 teaspoon sugar
- 1 teaspoon salt
- 1 tablespoon active dry yeast
- 1 cup warm water
- 2 tablespoons olive oil

For the Topping:

- 1/2 cup olive oil
- 1/2 cup za'atar spice mix

Instructions:

Preparing the Dough:

1. In a small bowl, combine warm water, sugar, and active dry yeast. Allow it to sit for 5-10 minutes, or until the mixture becomes frothy.

2. In a large mixing bowl, combine all-purpose flour and salt.
3. Make a well in the center of the flour mixture and pour in the yeast mixture and olive oil.
4. Mix the ingredients until a dough forms. Knead the dough on a floured surface for about 8-10 minutes, or until it becomes smooth and elastic.
5. Place the dough in a greased bowl, cover it with a damp cloth, and let it rise in a warm place for 1 hour, or until it doubles in size.

Shaping Zaatar Breadsticks:

1. Preheat the oven to 375°F (190°C).
2. Punch down the risen dough and divide it into 16 equal portions.
3. Roll each portion into a rope shape, about 8 inches long.
4. Place the shaped breadsticks on a baking sheet lined with parchment paper.

Topping Zaatar Breadsticks:

1. In a bowl, mix olive oil and za'atar spice mix.
2. Brush each breadstick generously with the za'atar and olive oil mixture, ensuring they are well-coated.

Baking Zaatar Breadsticks:

1. Bake in the preheated oven for 15-18 minutes, or until the breadsticks are golden brown.
2. Remove from the oven and let them cool on a wire rack.
3. Enjoy these flavorful and aromatic breadsticks as a snack or appetizer, perfect for dipping into olive oil or your favorite spreads!

LAHMACUN (TURKISH MEAT PIES)

Servings: 8 lahmacun
Time: 2 hours (including rising time)

Ingredients:

For the Dough:

- 4 cups all-purpose flour
- 1 teaspoon sugar
- 1 teaspoon salt
- 1 tablespoon active dry yeast
- 1 1/2 cups warm water
- 2 tablespoons olive oil

For the Meat Topping:

- 1 pound ground lamb or beef
- 1 large onion, finely chopped
- 2 tomatoes, finely chopped
- 1/2 cup fresh parsley, chopped
- 2 tablespoons tomato paste
- 2 tablespoons olive oil
- 2 teaspoons ground cumin
- 2 teaspoons ground paprika
- 1 teaspoon ground cinnamon
- Salt and black pepper to taste

For Serving:

- Fresh parsley, chopped
- Lemon wedges

Instructions:

Preparing the Dough:

1. In a small bowl, combine warm water, sugar, and active dry yeast. Allow it to sit for 5-10 minutes, or until the mixture becomes frothy.
2. In a large mixing bowl, combine all-purpose flour and salt.
3. Make a well in the center of the flour mixture and pour in the yeast mixture and olive oil.
4. Mix the ingredients until a dough forms. Knead the dough on a floured surface for about 8-10 minutes, or until it becomes smooth and elastic.
5. Place the dough in a greased bowl, cover it with a damp cloth, and let it rise in a warm place for 1 hour, or until it doubles in size.

Preparing the Meat Topping:

1. In a skillet, heat olive oil over medium heat.
2. Add finely chopped onions and cook until they are soft and translucent.
3. Add ground lamb or beef to the skillet and cook until browned.
4. Stir in chopped tomatoes, tomato paste, ground cumin, ground paprika, ground cinnamon, salt, and black pepper. Cook for an additional 5-7 minutes until the mixture is well combined.
5. Remove from heat and stir in fresh parsley.

Shaping Lahmacun:

1. Preheat the oven to 475°F (245°C).

2. Punch down the risen dough and divide it into 8 equal portions.
3. Roll each portion into a ball and let them rest for 10 minutes.
4. On a floured surface, roll out each ball into a thin round disc (about 8 inches in diameter).
5. Place the rolled-out dough on a baking sheet lined with parchment paper.

Assembling Lahmacun:

1. Spoon a generous amount of the meat topping onto each dough disc, spreading it evenly to the edges.
2. Bake in the preheated oven for 10-12 minutes, or until the edges are golden brown.
3. Remove from the oven and let the lahmacun cool slightly.
4. Sprinkle chopped fresh parsley over the top.
5. Serve warm with lemon wedges on the side.

CHEESE AND SPINACH FATAYER

Servings: 12 fatayer
Time: 2 hours (including rising time)

Ingredients:

For the Dough:

- 3 cups all-purpose flour
- 1 teaspoon sugar
- 1 teaspoon salt
- 1 tablespoon active dry yeast

- 1 cup warm water
- 2 tablespoons olive oil

For the Filling:

- 2 cups fresh spinach, chopped
- 1 cup feta cheese, crumbled
- 1/2 cup mozzarella cheese, shredded
- 1 small onion, finely chopped
- 2 tablespoons olive oil
- 1 teaspoon sumac (optional)
- Salt and black pepper to taste

Instructions:

Preparing the Dough:

1. In a small bowl, combine warm water, sugar, and active dry yeast. Allow it to sit for 5-10 minutes, or until the mixture becomes frothy.
2. In a large mixing bowl, combine all-purpose flour and salt.
3. Make a well in the center of the flour mixture and pour in the yeast mixture and olive oil.
4. Mix the ingredients until a dough forms. Knead the dough on a floured surface for about 8-10 minutes, or until it becomes smooth and elastic.
5. Place the dough in a greased bowl, cover it with a damp cloth, and let it rise in a warm place for 1 hour, or until it doubles in size.

Preparing the Filling:

1. In a skillet, heat olive oil over medium heat.

2. Add finely chopped onions and cook until they are soft and translucent.
3. Add chopped fresh spinach to the skillet and cook until it wilts.
4. In a bowl, combine cooked spinach and onions with crumbled feta cheese, shredded mozzarella cheese, sumac (if using), salt, and black pepper. Mix well.

Shaping Cheese and Spinach Fatayer:

1. Preheat the oven to 375°F (190°C).
2. Punch down the risen dough and divide it into 12 equal portions.
3. Roll each portion into a ball and let them rest for 10 minutes.
4. On a floured surface, roll out each ball into a small circle.
5. Place a spoonful of the cheese and spinach filling in the center of each circle.
6. Fold the edges of the dough over the filling, forming a triangle shape. Press the edges to seal.
7. Place the shaped fatayer on a baking sheet lined with parchment paper.

Baking Cheese and Spinach Fatayer:

1. Bake in the preheated oven for 15-18 minutes, or until the fatayer are golden brown.
2. Remove from the oven and let them cool on a wire rack.

DESSERTS AND SWEETS

LUQAIMAT (SWEET DUMPLINGS)

Servings: 6-8 servings
Time: 2 hours

Ingredients:

For the Dough:

- 2 cups all-purpose flour
- 1 teaspoon active dry yeast
- 1 tablespoon sugar
- 1/2 teaspoon baking powder
- 1/4 teaspoon salt
- 1 1/4 cups warm water

For the Sugar Syrup:

- 1 cup sugar
- 1/2 cup water
- 1 teaspoon lemon juice

For Frying:

- Vegetable oil for deep frying

For Garnish:

- Sesame seeds or ground pistachios (optional)

Instructions:

Preparing the Dough:

1. In a small bowl, combine warm water, sugar, and active dry yeast. Allow it to sit for 5-10 minutes, or until the mixture becomes frothy.
2. In a large mixing bowl, combine all-purpose flour, baking powder, and salt.
3. Make a well in the center of the flour mixture and pour in the yeast mixture.
4. Mix the ingredients until a smooth, thick batter forms.
5. Cover the bowl with a damp cloth and let the dough rise in a warm place for 1 hour.

Making the Sugar Syrup:

1. In a saucepan, combine sugar, water, and lemon juice.
2. Bring the mixture to a gentle boil, stirring until the sugar dissolves.

3. Simmer for 5-7 minutes, or until the syrup slightly thickens. Remove from heat and let it cool.

Frying Luqaimat:

1. Heat vegetable oil in a deep fryer or large, deep pan to 350°F (180°C).
2. Using two spoons or wet hands, drop small portions of the dough into the hot oil, forming rough ball shapes.
3. Fry until the luqaimat are golden brown and crispy on the outside. Make sure to turn them for even frying.
4. Remove the luqaimat from the oil and drain them on paper towels.

Coating Luqaimat:

1. While still warm, dip the luqaimat into the prepared sugar syrup, ensuring they are well-coated.
2. Arrange the coated luqaimat on a serving platter.

Garnishing (Optional):

1. Sprinkle sesame seeds or ground pistachios over the top for added texture and flavor.

BAKLAVA

Servings: 24 pieces
Time: 1.5 hours

Ingredients:

For the Filling:

- 2 cups walnuts, finely chopped
- 1 cup almonds, finely chopped
- 1/2 cup sugar
- 1 teaspoon ground cinnamon

For the Syrup:

- 1 cup water
- 1 cup sugar
- 1/2 cup honey
- 1 cinnamon stick
- 1 teaspoon lemon juice

For Assembling and Baking:

- 1 package phyllo dough (16 oz), thawed
- 1 cup unsalted butter, melted

Instructions:

Preparing the Filling:

1. In a bowl, combine finely chopped walnuts, almonds, sugar, and ground cinnamon. Mix well and set aside.

Making the Syrup:

1. In a saucepan, combine water, sugar, honey, cinnamon stick, and lemon juice.
2. Bring the mixture to a boil, then reduce the heat and simmer for 10-15 minutes, or until the syrup slightly thickens.
3. Remove the cinnamon stick and let the syrup cool.

Assembling and Baking:

1. Preheat the oven to 350°F (175°C).
2. Unroll the phyllo dough and cover it with a damp cloth to prevent drying.
3. Brush a baking dish with melted butter.
4. Place one sheet of phyllo dough in the dish and brush it with melted butter. Repeat with 7 more sheets, brushing each one with butter.
5. Sprinkle a generous portion of the nut filling evenly over the buttered phyllo layers.
6. Continue layering and buttering phyllo sheets, adding a layer of nuts every 8 sheets, until all the nut filling is used.
7. Finish with a top layer of 8 buttered phyllo sheets.
8. Using a sharp knife, cut the baklava into diamond or square shapes.
9. Bake in the preheated oven for 30-35 minutes, or until the baklava is golden brown and crisp.

Coating with Syrup:

1. Once out of the oven, immediately pour the cooled syrup evenly over the hot baklava.
2. Allow the baklava to absorb the syrup and cool completely in the dish.

UMM ALI

Servings: 6-8 servings
Time: 45 minutes

Ingredients:

- 4 cups croissants, torn into bite-sized pieces
- 2 cups whole milk
- 1 cup heavy cream
- 1/2 cup sugar
- 1/4 cup desiccated coconut
- 1/4 cup slivered almonds
- 1/4 cup raisins
- 1 teaspoon vanilla extract
- Pinch of ground cinnamon for garnish

Instructions:

1. **Preheat the Oven:** Preheat your oven to 350°F (175°C).
2. **Prepare the Croissants:** Tear the croissants into bite-sized pieces and spread them evenly in a baking dish.
3. **Prepare the Filling:** In a saucepan, heat the whole milk, heavy cream, and sugar over medium heat. Stir occasionally until the sugar dissolves and the mixture is warm but not boiling.
4. **Add Flavors:** Stir in the vanilla extract, desiccated coconut, slivered almonds, and raisins into the milk mixture.
5. **Pour over Croissants:** Pour the milk mixture over the torn croissants, ensuring they are well soaked.
6. **Bake in the Oven:** Place the baking dish in the preheated oven and bake for 25-30 minutes or until the top is golden brown, and the pudding is set.
7. **Garnish:** Once out of the oven, sprinkle a pinch of ground cinnamon over the top for extra flavor.
8. **Serve Warm:** Umm Ali is traditionally served warm. Allow it to cool for a few minutes before serving.

KUNAFA

Servings: 8-10 servings
Time: 1.5 hours

Ingredients:

For the Kunafa Dough:

- 1 pound kunafa dough (shredded phyllo dough)
- 1 cup unsalted butter, melted

For the Cheese Filling:

- 2 cups mozzarella cheese, shredded
- 1 cup ricotta cheese
- 1/2 cup sugar
- 1 teaspoon orange blossom water (optional)

For the Sugar Syrup:

- 1 cup sugar
- 1/2 cup water
- 1 teaspoon lemon juice
- 1 teaspoon rose water (optional)

For Garnish:

- Pistachios, chopped

Instructions:

Preparing the Kunafa Dough:

1. Preheat the oven to 350°F (175°C).

2. In a large bowl, separate the strands of kunafa dough, ensuring they are loose and airy.
3. Place half of the kunafa dough in a mixing bowl and drizzle half of the melted butter over it. Toss the kunafa strands gently to coat them with butter.
4. Grease a baking dish with butter and press the buttered kunafa dough into the bottom of the dish to create an even layer.
5. In a separate bowl, repeat the process with the remaining kunafa dough and melted butter. Set aside.

Preparing the Cheese Filling:

1. In a mixing bowl, combine shredded mozzarella cheese, ricotta cheese, sugar, and orange blossom water. Mix well until the ingredients are evenly incorporated.

Assembling Kunafa:

1. Spread the cheese filling evenly over the first layer of kunafa dough in the baking dish.
2. Place the second layer of buttered kunafa dough over the cheese filling, pressing it down gently.

Baking Kunafa:

1. Bake in the preheated oven for 30-35 minutes or until the kunafa is golden brown and crispy.

Making the Sugar Syrup:

1. In a saucepan, combine sugar, water, and lemon juice. Bring the mixture to a boil, then reduce the heat and

simmer for 10-15 minutes, or until the syrup slightly thickens.
2. Remove from heat and stir in rose water if using. Let the syrup cool.

Pouring the Sugar Syrup:

1. Once out of the oven, immediately pour the cooled sugar syrup evenly over the hot kunafa.

Garnishing:

1. Sprinkle chopped pistachios over the top for added texture and flavor.

ATAYEF (STUFFED PANCAKES)

Servings: 12-15 atayef
Time: 1.5 hours

Ingredients:

For the Atayef Dough:

- 2 cups all-purpose flour
- 1 teaspoon instant yeast
- 1 tablespoon sugar
- 1/2 teaspoon baking powder
- 2 cups warm water

For the Sweet Cheese Filling:

- 1 cup ricotta cheese
- 1/4 cup sugar

- 1 teaspoon orange blossom water (optional)

For the Nut Filling:

- 1 cup mixed nuts (walnuts, pistachios, almonds), finely chopped
- 1/4 cup sugar
- 1 teaspoon ground cinnamon
- 1 teaspoon rose water (optional)

For Frying:

- Vegetable oil for frying

For Garnish:

- Powdered sugar

Instructions:

Preparing the Atayef Dough:

1. In a mixing bowl, combine all-purpose flour, instant yeast, sugar, and baking powder.
2. Gradually add warm water while stirring until a smooth, lump-free batter forms. Cover the bowl with a damp cloth and let it rest for 30 minutes.

Making the Fillings:

Sweet Cheese Filling:

1. In a bowl, mix ricotta cheese, sugar, and orange blossom water (if using) until well combined. Set aside.

Nut Filling:

1. In another bowl, combine chopped mixed nuts, sugar, ground cinnamon, and rose water (if using). Set aside.

Filling and Folding Atayef:

1. Heat a non-stick skillet over medium-low heat.
2. Pour a small amount of batter onto the skillet to form small pancakes (about 3 inches in diameter).
3. Cook only on one side until the surface is covered with bubbles and the edges start to set.
4. Remove from the heat, and while the pancake is still soft and pliable, place a spoonful of either the sweet cheese or nut filling in the center.
5. Fold the pancake in half, pressing the edges to seal, creating a half-moon shape.

Frying Atayef:

1. Heat vegetable oil in a deep pan over medium heat.
2. Carefully place the stuffed atayef in the hot oil, seam side down.
3. Fry until both sides are golden brown. Remove and drain on paper towels.

Garnishing:

1. Dust the fried atayef with powdered sugar.

ASEEDA BOBAR (PUMPKIN DESSERT)

Servings: 6-8 servings
Time: 1.5 hours

Ingredients:

For the Aseeda:

- 2 cups pumpkin puree
- 1 cup barley flour
- 1 cup whole wheat flour
- 1/2 cup unsalted butter, melted
- 1/2 cup honey or to taste
- 1/2 teaspoon ground cinnamon
- 1/4 teaspoon ground nutmeg
- Pinch of salt

For the Sauce:

- 1/4 cup unsalted butter
- 1/4 cup honey
- 1/4 cup water
- 1 teaspoon ground cinnamon
- Chopped nuts for garnish (optional)

Instructions:

Preparing the Aseeda:

1. In a large mixing bowl, combine pumpkin puree, barley flour, whole wheat flour, melted butter, honey, ground cinnamon, ground nutmeg, and a pinch of salt.
2. Mix the ingredients until a smooth dough forms. It should have a thick consistency.
3. Grease a round mold or a plate with butter.

4. Press the aseeda dough into the mold or plate, smoothing the top with a spatula.
5. Allow the aseeda to set and cool for about 30 minutes.

Making the Sauce:

1. In a saucepan, combine butter, honey, water, and ground cinnamon.
2. Heat the mixture over medium heat, stirring until the butter is melted, and the sauce is well combined.
3. Remove the sauce from heat and let it cool slightly.

Serving:

1. Once the aseeda is set and cooled, drizzle the cinnamon honey sauce over the top.
2. Optionally, garnish with chopped nuts.
3. Cut into wedges and serve Aseeda Bobar at room temperature.

DATE AND NUT ROLL

Servings: 12-15 slices
Time: 1 hour

Ingredients:

For the Date and Nut Filling:

• 2 cups dates, pitted and chopped
• 1 cup mixed nuts (walnuts, almonds, pistachios), finely chopped
• 1/4 cup desiccated coconut

- 1 teaspoon ground cinnamon
- 1/4 teaspoon ground nutmeg
- 1 tablespoon honey

For the Outer Layer:

- 1 cup mixed nuts (walnuts, almonds, pistachios), finely chopped
- 1/4 cup desiccated coconut

For Rolling:

- Powdered sugar for dusting

Instructions:

Preparing the Date and Nut Filling:

1. In a food processor, combine chopped dates, mixed nuts, desiccated coconut, ground cinnamon, ground nutmeg, and honey.
2. Pulse the mixture until it forms a sticky and well-combined filling.

Assembling the Date and Nut Roll:

1. Lay out a piece of plastic wrap on a flat surface.
2. Spread the date and nut filling onto the plastic wrap, forming a rectangle shape.
3. Roll the filling tightly using the plastic wrap to shape it into a log.
4. In a separate bowl, combine finely chopped mixed nuts and desiccated coconut.

5. Unwrap the date and nut log and roll it in the nut and coconut mixture, ensuring it is coated evenly.

Chilling and Setting:

1. Wrap the coated log in plastic wrap again and refrigerate for at least 30 minutes to allow it to set.

Serving:

1. Once set, remove from the refrigerator and dust with powdered sugar.
2. Slice into rounds and serve the Date and Nut Roll.

ROZ BEL LABAN (RICE PUDDING)

Servings: 4-6 servings
Time: 1 hour

Ingredients:

- 1/2 cup short-grain rice
- 4 cups whole milk
- 1/2 cup sugar or to taste
- 1 teaspoon vanilla extract
- Ground cinnamon for garnish
- Chopped nuts (almonds or pistachios) for garnish

Instructions:

Cooking the Rice:

1. Rinse the short-grain rice under cold water until the water runs clear.

2. In a saucepan, combine the rinsed rice and 2 cups of water. Bring to a boil, then reduce the heat, cover, and simmer until the rice is cooked and water is absorbed (about 15-20 minutes).

Making the Rice Pudding:

1. Add 4 cups of whole milk to the cooked rice in the saucepan.
2. Bring the mixture to a gentle simmer over medium heat, stirring frequently to prevent the rice from sticking to the bottom.
3. Once the mixture is simmering, reduce the heat to low and continue to cook, stirring occasionally, until the rice is soft and the mixture thickens (about 30-40 minutes).
4. Add sugar to the rice and milk mixture, stirring continuously until the sugar dissolves.
5. Stir in vanilla extract and continue to cook for an additional 5-10 minutes, or until the rice pudding reaches your desired consistency.

Serving:

1. Remove the rice pudding from heat and let it cool slightly.
2. Spoon the rice pudding into serving bowls.
3. Sprinkle ground cinnamon over the top for flavor and a touch of warmth.
4. Garnish with chopped nuts, such as almonds or pistachios, for added texture.

Chilling (Optional):

1. For a chilled version, refrigerate the rice pudding for a few hours before serving.

SAFFRON AND CARDAMOM ICE CREAM

Servings: 6-8 servings
Time: 4 hours (including freezing time)

Ingredients:

- 2 cups heavy cream
- 1 cup whole milk
- 1 cup granulated sugar
- 1/2 teaspoon saffron threads
- 1 teaspoon ground cardamom
- 1 teaspoon vanilla extract
- Pinch of salt
- Chopped pistachios for garnish (optional)

Instructions:

Infusing Saffron:

1. In a small bowl, crush saffron threads with your fingers.
2. In a small saucepan, heat 1/4 cup of heavy cream over low heat. Add crushed saffron threads to the warm cream and let it steep for 15-20 minutes. This will infuse the saffron flavor into the cream.
3. After steeping, strain the saffron-infused cream to remove the saffron threads.

Making the Ice Cream Base:

1. In a mixing bowl, combine the remaining heavy cream, whole milk, granulated sugar, ground cardamom, vanilla extract, and a pinch of salt.
2. Add the saffron-infused cream to the mixture and whisk until the sugar is completely dissolved.

Chilling the Mixture:

1. Cover the bowl with plastic wrap and refrigerate the ice cream mixture for at least 2 hours or overnight to chill thoroughly.

Freezing the Ice Cream:

1. Once the mixture is chilled, pour it into an ice cream maker.
2. Follow the manufacturer's instructions to churn the ice cream until it reaches a soft-serve consistency.
3. Transfer the churned ice cream to a lidded container, spreading it evenly.
4. Cover the container with a lid and freeze for at least 2 hours, or until the ice cream is firm.

Serving:

1. Scoop the Saffron and Cardamom Ice Cream into bowls or cones.
2. Optionally, garnish with chopped pistachios for added flavor and texture.

BASBOUSA (SEMOLINA CAKE)

Servings: 12-15 pieces
Time: 1 hour

Ingredients:

For the Cake:

- 2 cups semolina
- 1 cup granulated sugar
- 1 cup plain yogurt
- 1/2 cup unsalted butter, melted
- 1 teaspoon baking powder
- 1/4 cup desiccated coconut (optional)
- 1 teaspoon vanilla extract
- 1/4 cup blanched almonds or whole pine nuts for garnish

For the Sugar Syrup:

- 1 cup granulated sugar
- 1/2 cup water
- 1 tablespoon lemon juice
- 1 teaspoon rose water (optional)

Instructions:

Making the Cake:

1. Preheat the oven to 350°F (175°C). Grease a baking dish or line it with parchment paper.
2. In a mixing bowl, combine semolina, sugar, yogurt, melted butter, baking powder, desiccated coconut (if using), and vanilla extract. Mix until well combined.
3. Allow the mixture to rest for 10-15 minutes, allowing the semolina to absorb the liquid.

4. Pour the batter into the prepared baking dish, spreading it evenly.
5. Score the top of the batter into diamond or square shapes with a knife.
6. Place a blanched almond or a pine nut in the center of each scored piece.

Baking the Basbousa:

1. Bake in the preheated oven for 30-35 minutes or until the top is golden brown and a toothpick inserted into the center comes out clean.

Making the Sugar Syrup:

1. In a saucepan, combine sugar, water, and lemon juice. Bring the mixture to a boil, stirring until the sugar dissolves.
2. Simmer the syrup for 10-15 minutes or until it slightly thickens.
3. Remove from heat and stir in rose water if using. Let the syrup cool.

Pouring the Sugar Syrup:

1. Once the basbousa is out of the oven, immediately pour the cooled sugar syrup evenly over the hot cake.

Soaking:

1. Allow the basbousa to absorb the syrup for at least 30 minutes before serving.

MEASUREMENT CONVERSIONS

Volume Conversions:

- 1 cup = 8 fluid ounces = 240 milliliters
- 1 tablespoon = 3 teaspoons = 15 milliliters
- 1 fluid ounce = 2 tablespoons = 30 milliliters
- 1 quart = 4 cups = 32 fluid ounces = 946 milliliters
- 1 gallon = 4 quarts = 128 fluid ounces = 3.78 liters
- 1 liter = 1,000 milliliters = 33.8 fluid ounces
- 1 milliliter = 0.034 fluid ounces = 0.002 cups

Weight Conversions:

- 1 pound = 16 ounces = 453.592 grams
- 1 ounce = 28.349 grams
- 1 gram = 0.035 ounces = 0.001 kilograms
- 1 kilogram = 1,000 grams = 35.274 ounces = 2.205 pounds

Temperature Conversions:

- To convert from Fahrenheit to Celsius: (°F - 32) / 1.8
- To convert from Celsius to Fahrenheit: (°C * 1.8) + 32

Length Conversions:

- 1 inch = 2.54 centimeters
- 1 foot = 12 inches = 30.48 centimeters
- 1 yard = 3 feet = 36 inches = 91.44 centimeters
- 1 meter = 100 centimeters = 1.094 yards.

Made in United States
Orlando, FL
09 April 2025